THE COMMONSENSE GARDENER

STEFAN BUCZACKI

FRANCES LINCOLN

THE COMMONSENSE
GARDENER
STEFAN BUCZACKI

4 Torriano Mews
Torriano Avenue
London NW5 2RZ
www.franceslincoln.com

British Library Cataloguing-in-Publication data
A catalogue record for this book is available from the
British Library

ISBN 0 7112 2264 9

Printed and bound in Singapore by Tien Wah Press

9 8 7 6 5 4 3 2 1

CONTENTS

GENERAL
PRINCIPLES

GENERAL PRINCIPLES

It wasn't anything deliberate on my part. I didn't sit down one day with the notion and intention of formulating a gardening philosophy. Rather, it happened by default. Increasingly, at the end of lectures, in correspondence or in chance meetings in gardens and at gardening events, I became aware that people were telling me they enjoyed listening to what I said and reading what I wrote because it seemed to be common sense. I wasn't driven by dogma, nor was I recycling what other people had said or written. I have never been a slavish follower of fashions or trends; I have sometimes been accused of deliberately going against them although I don't think that's true. But I have always believed strongly in learning by experience and by making mistakes.

No one ever showed me how to garden. As a child, I watched and helped my father and uncle, both keen and enthusiastic amateur gardeners, and I clearly absorbed much by their example. My professional qualifications are in botany and forestry; my professional experience largely in the field of commercial horticulture. And, like most people, I didn't garden on a regular basis until we bought our first house, in 1970. But I soon realized that much of what my colleagues and I were studying for the good of commercial vegetable growers was of considerable interest and relevance to gardeners too. So I began to give talks to gardening societies, to contribute to the popular gardening press, to write books for gardeners and, by 1980, to appear on television and radio. This wasn't popular with my employers, who took the view then that serious scientific research wasn't to be sullied by contact with mere amateur gardeners. How times change; their successors today fall over backwards to have the general public on their side as they regularly lock horns with their paymasters seeking more research funding.

As I came to know the gardening fraternity more, I continued to develop the highest respect for them and for the fund of horticultural knowledge that resides in the British population, perhaps to a greater extent than anywhere else. And they began to teach me. By seeing more gardens and meeting more gardeners in the course of a year than most people, I absorbed this collective learning and added to my own knowledge and experience. I began to call the way I gardened and the way I taught the subject 'commonsense gardening'. It's an approach that can be applied to every gardening operation but its benefits are more evident in certain areas than others. I will begin by looking at some aspects of gardening in which I feel it is especially relevant.

ORGANIC GARDENING

I am often asked if I consider myself to be an organic gardener; and also if commonsense gardening is the same as organic gardening. The answer to the first is 'Insofar as it makes sense to me'; and to the second 'Yes, but without the dogma'. Organic gardening is as much about words and definitions as about horticulture and two words that have caught and gripped the imagination of the gardening public over recent years are 'green' and 'organic'. But, as so often happens with rediscovered vocabulary, their meanings have changed slightly from what was previously intended or understood. The word 'green' has quite clearly taken on a whole new socio-political significance, while 'organic', according to the relevant dictionary definitions, simply means 'relating to, derived from, or characteristic of plants and animals' or 'belonging to the class of chemical compounds that are

formed from carbon'. Of these, it tends to be the former that carries more weight in the horticultural fraternity. A belief has grown up that garden chemicals 'derived from plants and animals' are safer, better or otherwise more desirable than those from other sources. And therein lies a problem. Those chemicals that happen to have had a 'natural' origin or started life somewhere other than in a chemical factory have nothing of real importance in common. It makes about as much scientific sense to group together bone meal and derris as it does strychnine and orange juice.

I stand by a remark about organic gardening I first made some years ago and which has aroused the odd comment since. I believe all good gardeners can be, and generally are, essentially organic gardeners. You don't need to run a flag to the top of a pole to announce the fact to the world; nor do you need to cover your garden with old carpet and polythene sheet and surround it with the waste products of the local tyre depot. My organic gardening has nothing to do with abiding by someone else's rulebook about chemicals or being hypocritical about the use of plastic. It has a great deal, however, to do with wanting to garden in harmony with the environment and with wanting to enjoy the hobby as productively as possible while living in a state of mutual contentment with as many wild creatures as possible.

Upturned plant pots filled with straw make simple and effective traps for earwigs.

On my travels I meet many gardeners, a fair proportion of whom preface their questions to me with an organic comment. But they tend not to say anything as cut and dried as 'I am an organic gardener'. The comment tends to be more along the lines of 'I'm not keen on using chemicals if I can avoid it', or 'I try to be as organic as possible'. This confirms my belief that most gardeners already have a great deal of common sense. They aren't going to obey slavishly someone on the television who tells them they must do it this way or that.

Organic gardening is approached in different ways by different gardeners, even given my broader definition of the term. My experience tells me the ones who are least devoted to the organic doctrine are older vegetable gardeners with allotments. They want the best yield from their plots and if it means using, as an elderly neighbour

Horticultural fleece will protect brassicas from large white butterflies as effectively as it will carrots from carrot fly.

of mine puts it, 'a little bit of the artificial', then so be it. Perhaps surprisingly, the second least likely to adhere to organic principles closely are those younger gardeners who have had their gardens for around five years. What seems to happen is that, with their first flush of enthusiasm for the new plot, they have high-flown ideas about doing their bit to save the planet. Chemicals, both good and bad, it seems, are shunned and a supposedly clean-living doctrine of horticulture is embraced. Yet before long, it becomes clear that know-how has been in short supply, so the compost hasn't materialized in quite the way it was intended. Experience has also been lacking, so the most appropriate varieties may not have been chosen and they may not have been planted in the most efficient and productive way. By and large, by year four or five, that imagined care for the planet is on the wane. That is when organic gardening goes out of the window and easy, carefree, buy-it-in-a-packet gardening takes over.

Make no mistake; organic gardening isn't easy gardening. Learning takes time, materials take time to accumulate and there is much more trial and error to contend with than there is with 'artificial' gardening. And it's for these reasons too you don't see much organic gardening in those small inner city gardens owned and run by busy people who just don't have time to spare and yet want 'things to look nice'. And of course, the paucity of real organic matter in any inner city can make decent organic gardening there an expensive proposition.

I saw the cost of bagged 'organic manure' in a garden centre in Chelsea recently and felt extremely pleased to live in the country.

For if one thing underlies organic gardening, it is organic matter. Time and again on travelling radio and television programmes around the UK, when I have been asked about soil improvement, I have found myself asking 'How easy is it to obtain manure in this area?' And there are many parts of the country, including many rural areas, where the answer is 'Not easy at all because we no longer have any cows or horses'. The most profitable farming in the country today is characterized by a landscape of wide, open spaces, with scarcely a beast for miles. I was appalled to be told by a gardener from just such an agricultural area recently that even such horse manure as there is (from riding stables) tends to be burned for want of something better to do with it. This is sacrilege,

Shredded and composted bark mulch not only retains soil moisture but also limits annual weed growth.

born, it seems, from people simply forgetting what real gardening is all about. But this story appears to carry the message that, like it or not, in many parts of the country, gardening merely mirrors what farming does. All the more reason for turning every gram of waste organic debris into compost. But how many of us do?

I was paying one of my occasional visits to our local waste tip the other day. It's all rather well organized, with separate places to leave old washing machines, deposit waste oil, dump newspapers, green bottles, brown bottles, plastic and so forth. And then there are several big skips. 'Please Use This Skip' is written on large notices attached to the two already overflowing with rubbish, while 'Please Do NOT Use This Skip' is attached to the empty ones. But that wasn't really what concerned me. I was far more distressed to see a large skip with the notice 'Green Garden Rubbish Only'. A man in front of me had a small trailer behind his car and was unloading bag after bag of garden waste, including several bags that contained nothing more than leaves. I wished I had had room in the back of my car, as I would gladly have carried the entire contents home with me. Or I could have hitched his trailer to my own tow bar and saved him the effort.

I expect that people like the man with the trailer – who have filled the garden skip with their old prunings, herbaceous trimmings, lawn mowings and the rest – will call in at the garden centre on their way home to pay handsomely for bags of

it isn't the fact that it chops wood that makes it so useful. It is simply the fact that it chops. Even relatively soft herbaceous material will decompose better when it is slashed into smaller fragments because the greater the surface area in relation to the weight, the more effectively and quickly the bacteria and fungi in your compost bin will be able to decompose them. There are many models on the market, most powered by electricity but some, especially the largest, with petrol engines. The bigger, most powerful machines are fairly expensive but price isn't usually a prohibiting factor for people who hesitate over a purchase. Nor are running costs. There are two things that really concern people. The noise these machines generate is one of them. In some countries noise pollution is taken so seriously that there are restrictions on the times in the week that powered garden machinery of any sort may be used. I don't deny that shredders are noisy although legislation in Europe and in the United States means that noise reduction is now the most important factor for the manufacturers; with quieter (and more efficient) engines and various ingenious sound deadening devices, modern machines are immeasurably less intrusive than their predecessors. But legislation or not, I would still urge all gardeners to use them on days and at times when they will cause the least offence to neighbours. Try to shred small quantities regularly, rather than allowing waste to accumulate and then finding you require all day to deal with it.

proprietary organic 'planting medium', 'soil conditioner' and the like. What has happened to recycling and compost and leaf-mould making? In part I think I know.

You can't make good compost, and you certainly can't use all the waste from any except the smallest garden, without a compost shredder. It will chop up almost all woody garden debris but

A shredder makes much sense – it enables almost all garden waste to be composted, although some may consume as much energy as they save.

The second concern often expressed about shredders is a more fundamental one, a serious environmental objection to them on the premise that they use up more energy shredding waste matter than they provide in additional compost. I think that in purely arithmetical terms, and within your own garden, this may be true. But what of the energy that would be expended if you didn't make use of it? Someone would have to take the waste from your garden and it would probably end up, like that in the man's trailer at our local tip, being put to no useful function and simply being buried in the ground.

I currently have eight compost bins, five of which are used for making compost and three are for leaf mould. It makes sense to keep the two materials separate because leaves decompose much more slowly than other organic matter and if they are mixed with everything else, they tend to form a compact mat which blocks the flow of water and air through the whole. Putting leaves through the shredder certainly helps, however, especially with large or tough types such as horse chestnut or holly, if you have time to do it. Adequate aeration and correct moisture content are critical for good compost making and that is why my compost is made in bins – wooden bins with slatted sides. There are people who claim to make good compost in fully enclosed structures, even in holes in the ground. Good luck to them. I can't manage it and I don't understand how the process operates because the micro-organisms that do the work are aerobic – they require oxygen to function properly. Deny air to the waste matter and you will encourage other bacteria, anaerobic organisms, that will bring about a different degradation of organic matter, resulting in the formation of an amorphous dark material and the production of noxious gases – commonly a mixture of foul-smelling hydrogen sulphide, hydrogen and methane.

PRUNING

Pruning is among the most important routine gardening tasks where a commonsense approach pays dividends, saving you time and giving you better results. It is still perhaps the least understood of all basic gardening tasks; yet, with common sense, the mysterious is transformed into the totally logical. But trying to explain to someone how to prune is a futile exercise unless you are sure they understand why pruning is done and how it works. Then they will understand both how to prune, how severely to prune and when (and when not) to do it.

The severity of pruning all woody flowering and fruiting plants is dictated by plant vigour, whereas the season in which the pruning should be performed is closely influenced by flowering time. Let's first consider vigour. A growth-suppressing chemical is produced in the apical bud at the tip of a plant's stem and this travels downwards inside the tissues, preventing the lower buds from growing and so ensuring the stem elongates upwards. But if you cut off the end of the shoot, you will remove that bud, remove the suppressing chemical and so

stimulate buds further down the shoot to burst into life. This is why regular clipping of a hedge will thicken its overall growth. A similar effect results when a shoot is bent downwards approximately to the horizontal, rather than being cut off. This technique is especially valuable when you want the lower parts of a wall clothed with a climbing rose or when fruit trees are producing excessively long shoots but few accessible fruit.

The more of the main shoot you remove, the greater the stimulation of the side shoot growth. And the greater the severity with which these are in turn cut back, the greater the proliferation of overall shoot growth. The practical consequence is that severe (or, as it is usually called, hard) pruning should be used in order to help encourage more growth from a plant that is growing feebly or is inherently of weak constitution. Conversely, a strongly growing plant should in general be pruned lightly in order to contain its vigour. These differences apply as much to individual plant varieties as they do to species – a strongly growing and vigorous cluster-flowered (Floribunda) rose such as 'Queen Elizabeth', for instance, should be pruned much more lightly than a weaker growing variety such as 'Korresia'.

LEFT: The apical bud produces chemicals that control the growth of other buds further down the shoot. RIGHT: Marginally hardy plants (like hydrangeas in many areas) are best pruned in the spring – the old shoots help protect the crown against winter frost.

The timing of pruning is also governed by simple considerations. Flowering shrubs bear their flowers in one of two ways – either on the shoots produced during the current year or on those produced in the previous or earlier years. Generally, plants that flower in the first half of the year do so on the previous year's growth; those that flower in the second half do so on the current season's shoots. There is no alternative. In order not to cut away the new flower buds therefore, early-flowering shrubs should be pruned immediately after they have flowered and generally these require light pruning. Those plants that flower later in the season should be pruned some time between the end of flowering and the beginning of the next year's growth in early spring. Proportionately more of the later-flowering plants benefit from hard pruning and, in the case of those plants that are only marginally hardy in many areas (hydrangeas and outdoor fuchsias for example), the operation is better left until the spring because

the old shoots will give added protection to the crown of the plants against the damaging effects of winter cold.

FEEDING

I now want to turn my attention to plant feeding, another enduring mystery to many gardeners who realize they need to do it but commonly with little understanding of the principles or of how to select a fertilizer. Common sense will help here too. There are well over a hundred chemical elements known to exist on earth but plants require only a small number of them. The most important are nitrogen, phosphorus and potassium – generally called the major nutrients – followed by calcium, magnesium, iron, manganese, copper, molybdenum, sodium, zinc, chlorine and sulphur. Most of the latter, however, are required in extremely small amounts and are known as trace elements. For most gardening purposes, you can forget about everything except nitrogen, phosphorus and potassium. Nitrogen is the most important plant nutrient because it is a major constituent of protein, protoplasm and other plant components, and is also incorporated into many other organic chemical compounds. It is always associated with leafy growth rather than flower and fruit development; too much nitrogen can

Nodules on the roots of plants in the pea and bean family conain nitrogen 'fixing' bacteria that enhance the nitrogen content of the soil.

delay or even inhibit flowering, something that comes a surprise to a gardener thinking that simply putting on more fertilizer will inevitably make all things right.

The main natural source of nitrogen is dead organic matter but it is uniquely different from all other soil elements in that it also passes into the soil from the air in mineral form. The roots of some plants, especially those in the pea and bean family, bear small bacteria-containing nodules and these bacteria live in symbiotic relationship with the plants. The process, called nitrogen fixation, involves in part the formation of ammonia and amino acids but ultimately the nitrogen finds its way into the soil in a form that can be used directly by plants. This is why crop rotation plans invariably advise growing crops like brassicas after peas and beans – because they are grown mainly to produce leaves not flowers, and they require a large amount of nitrogen. But nitrogen is highly soluble and

disappears rapidly from the soil by leaching so almost any soil will become nitrogen deficient after repeated cropping. It needs more replenishment than any other garden fertilizer element; and that is why, when choosing a fertilizer, you should check first how much nitrogen it contains. I'll return to that in a moment but let's now look at the other two important elements, phosphorus and potassium.

Phosphorus (usually referred to as phosphate, which is simply the form in which phosphorus is used by plants) is involved in many aspects of plant growth and is a constituent of numerous carbohydrates, proteins and fats. It has a special importance in the ripening of fruits and in the ripening and germination of seeds and its importance for encouraging root growth has been known for decades. This is why fertilizers like bone meal containing a high proportion of phosphate are so valuable when planting perennials.

Potassium (or potash) is of great importance for encouraging flower and fruit development even though it's not fully known how it works. So if your flowers aren't flowering or your fruit aren't fruiting, it's to increasing the amount of potash that you should turn.

When you buy fertilizer, you will find somewhere on the container a formula with the letters N, P and K in it, followed by numbers, along the lines of 5:5:12 or 8:8:10. These indicate the percentage amounts of each nutrient, always in the order nitrogen, phosphate, potash. The lower the numbers, the more fertilizer you must add to achieve a given result but if, as is generally the case, the amounts of all three nutrients are important, remember that the *relative* proportions are more significant than their *absolute* amounts. A fertilizer of composition 2:2:5, for example, is relatively just as rich in potassium as one of 8:8:20; you will simply require four times as much of it to give your plants the same amounts of nutrients.

For me, the essence of organic gardening is properly confined to the recycling of organic matter but the topic has spilled over into a consideration of garden chemical usage and to the choice between organic and inorganic fertilizers. An organic fertilizer is one derived from some living or once living organism and it therefore contrasts with an inorganic fertilizer which originates in some other way, usually, although not necessarily, an artificial manufacturing process. Why should you choose one over the other? What are the differences? Is there a commonsense approach to this?

Most inorganic fertilizers have a rather precise composition whereas most organic ones don't, although this doesn't have much practical significance in gardens. Most inorganic fertilizers don't contain any minor elements in addition to their major nutrients although this too is hardly ever significant in gardens where minor elements are seldom lacking – few soils in Britain are deficient in minor nutrients. Most inorganic fertilizers are highly soluble and therefore fairly fast acting, which means they won't last all season and need regular topping up, although the development of coated

fertilizer granules or pellets in recent years has added a controlled solubility and controlled release capability to the inorganic options too. (I'm often asked about the tiny spherical fertilizer balls in the compost of pot plants, which are commonly believed to be slug eggs.) Conversely, while most organic fertilizers are more insoluble and slower acting (or as it is often called, slower release), some can be rendered fairly fast acting if they are ground to a fine powder which increases the particle surface area and hence the solubility. There's not a great deal here therefore to help your choice.

Understandably and rightly, all gardeners today are aware of the need to minimize contamination and destruction of the natural environment and it is on the use of fertilizers in particular that much of conservationists' venom has been directed in

Raspberries, especially when growing in alkaline conditions, are among the relatively few plants that commonly show symptoms of iron deficiency.

recent years. There can be serious contamination of the environment in general and of water supplies in particular by excessive usage of artificial nitrogenous fertilizers on the land. The use of artificial fertilizers in gardens accounts for only a minute amount of the total consumption in the UK (which is about 1.5 million tonnes of nitrogen annually) but that is no reason for us not to be careful. I don't believe it argues against gardeners using artificial fertilizers but it does argue against using more than is necessary. There is still too widespread a belief that the more fertilizer you add, the better. It isn't; for every use of garden fertilizer there is an optimum.

The second environmental aspect of fertilizer usage that attracts opprobrium relates not to its application to the land but to its removal from it through mining or quarrying operations and, to some degree, to its manufacture. And despite what is sometimes claimed, there really are no fertilizers that escape all of these criticisms. Fertilizers produced by straightforward chemistry in a factory clearly contribute to a despoiling, if not direct pollution of the environment in the vicinity of the factory; the immediate surroundings of almost any large fertilizer factory present an unappealing vision. But it makes no sense to me to condemn them on these grounds without also taking account of the appalling devastation of Pacific Ocean islands and South American sea-bird colonies brought about by the production of 'organic' fertilizers like rock phosphate or guano. And I would guess that most of those gardeners (and I am one of them) who prefer to rely for their plants' nutrients on dried blood, bone meal and hoof and horn have never seen the inside of a slaughterhouse. I'm not taking sides or making a moral judgment, just putting a balanced, commonsense case.

The aspect of the choice between organic and inorganic fertilizers that has always intrigued me most, however, relates to their relative effects on the flavour of vegetables and other edible garden produce. Vegetables grown from organic fertilizers taste better, I am often told, despite the fact that plants make use of fertilizers not in the chemical form in which we provide them but after they have been converted to more basic components. Nitrogen to a plant is nitrogen, whether it originates in ammonium sulphate or in dried blood. Taste is, of course, a subjective matter and if you can detect a difference, all well and good; it may have some basis in scientific fact yet the evidence is strangely lacking. And in view of the diverse chemical processes that go to make up that curious phenomenon called flavour, I am always astonished, not so much that the type of fertilizer can affect it, but that an organic fertilizer should always change it in ways that we consider an improvement. It doesn't sound to me like common sense.

But having said all of that, I much prefer to eat produce from my own kitchen garden where I have used garden compost and organic fertilizers; and, more importantly, I do believe the flavour is

much better. But my scientific common sense tells me that fertilizers are only part of the taste story. It is probably more important that the produce is absolutely fresh and that, by and large, I grow varieties with an innately fine flavour because I'm not constrained by such commercial considerations as them having a high and uniform yield, beautiful appearance or the ability to remain for several days on a supermarket shelf.

PESTS, DISEASES AND WEEDS

Does the commonsense approach tell us much about the control of pests, diseases and weeds and about the use of garden pesticides? It does, and as much as anything, I think it tells us that horticultural hypochondria is an easy and unnecessary condition in which to become

Although I use organic fertilizer for my potatoes, I'm not convinced that it really improves their already excellent flavour.

trapped. Most garden plant pests and diseases need no treatment. I say this because they either cause only slight or cosmetic damage or a perfectly acceptable level of crop loss. Take one of the commonest of all garden diseases: brown rot of apples, which causes the familiar soft brown decay accompanied by concentric rings of fungal spore pustules on apples. Every year I am probably asked more questions about this disease than about any other – what can be done, can it be controlled and so forth. The short answers are no, it can't be controlled, and only a small amount can be done to prevent it. If you pick off and destroy the affected fruit and make sure no old fruit are left hanging on the tree over winter, you

might make a slight impact but it will only be slight because the disease is present in everyone else's garden and spores will blow from theirs to yours next season. More to the point, just look at how many healthy apples there are in your garden, on your trees. Unless the tree is only one year old and bearing its first, eagerly anticipated crop, I don't believe the loss to brown rot of some, even many, even most, of the fruit will really be a disaster.

There's no place in the garden for trying to obtain a 100 per cent healthy result. Neither is there any place in the garden (or anywhere else) for cosmetic horticulture, for trying to obtain flowers, foliage, fruit or vegetables that are blemish-free. It's a pointless and stupid doctrine that can be laid at the feet of the supermarkets who have encouraged a generation to grow up believing this is the way produce must always appear.

Do I use sprays in my own garden? Yes, but not every year and only three at most – against large white butterfly caterpillars (on nasturtiums rather more than brassicas), against aphids and against rose black spot. So if chemical controls of pests and diseases are required, is there a logical and commonsense approach to selecting them? Yes, and it simply depends on knowing a little about the different types of chemical, the effects they have and the ways they achieve them.

Brown rot on apples and other fruit simply has to be tolerated – it is extremely common and nothing will significantly reduce its impact.

Fungicides and insecticides are almost all relatively harmless to plant life so there's no real need to be concerned on that basis. The only significant exception to this was the mixture of tar oils sold as a winter wash for killing overwintering pests on dormant deciduous trees. This product has recently been withdrawn, although the use of it against one particular pest demonstrated rather neatly another facet of the commonsense approach to gardening.

Woolly aphid on apples can be a scourge, less for the effect it has on yield than for the appalling mess that it causes. The sticky white woolly wax secreted by the insects is unavoidably transferred on to clothes when the trees are being pruned or when anyone brushes past them. And as it is most serious on closely pruned and trained plants, such as cordons or espaliers, against which people do brush, it can be a real nuisance. Insecticide sprays used during the summer have little effect, however, because the woolly wax serves its purpose and the chemical rolls off leaving the insects unharmed beneath. Logically, tar oil sprayed in the winter ought to have worked but it too had little impact. The answer lies in knowing where the pests spend the dormant season. Most of them are tucked safely away in hard swollen galls on the twigs, produced by the trees in response to the infestation. Be ruthless and use robust secateurs to cut these out when doing your winter pruning and you will master the problem within a season.

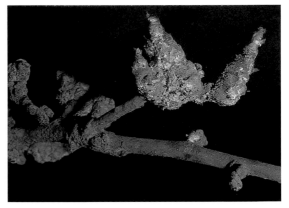

But to return to chemicals and other factors to take into account: first, and perhaps most obvious but often overlooked, is that chemicals designed to control pests won't control diseases; chemicals to control diseases won't control pests; and chemicals to control weeds won't do either. In most cases, it's fairly obvious which problem is which, although admittedly there are some slightly confusing instances – a few pests, such as the woolly aphid pictured above, can look rather like a mould. It's fairly obvious too which chemical is which, although there can still be confusion. A few years ago, a chemical company wanting to create an identifiable overall branding for its products introduced the prefix 'Tumble-' for them – Tumblebug to control pests, Tumbleblite to control diseases and Tumbleweed to control weeds. But

Knowing that apple woolly aphids spend the winter in these hard galls offers an obvious means of control – cut them off.

a surprising number of people have told me that although they remembered the 'Tumble-', they hadn't thought too carefully about the rest, and the consequences if they had used the weed killer for a pest or disease could have been unfortunate. I would prefer the names to be rather more unambiguous but this does underline the importance of reading labels carefully.

If I had been writing this a few years ago, I would now be discussing in some detail the choice between systemic and non-systemic products, a systemic chemical being one that is absorbed by a plant and moved within its tissues, as opposed to a non-systemic substance, which is not, or only slightly, and remains more or less where it is applied on the surface. In theory, systemic chemicals should be better for controlling diseases that are deeply entrenched in the tissues or pests that suck the sap. In practice, there are now so few pesticide and fungicide chemicals still approved for gardeners to buy (although there are several different brands of each) that I am sure you will use whatever is available. Weed killers, however, are importantly different. Most of the weed killers that have any effect on the control of serious perennial weeds such as bindweed, couch grass or ground elder are quite unsuitable for use in areas that are to be replanted within the medium term as they work by persisting in the soil for long periods. This is why some of them are used for the treatment of paths and other non-planted areas. There is, however, one important systemic (or translocated as it is sometimes called) weed killer called glyphosate. This has a special and valuable role to play in the garden as it offers the only reliable and effective means of eradicating deep-seated perennial weeds while leaving the soil uncontaminated for planting immediately afterwards.

I have said that my comments on chemicals would have been different a few years ago. My overall approach to the treatment of pests would have been different too because we really are now at a stage where direct control needn't mean chemicals. Biological control of pests has at last come of age in the home garden (although there is still no biological control of diseases). Using one creature to control another isn't new – the Chinese were doing it centuries ago and it has been a standard technique in commercial horticulture for some time. Only recently, however, have production and distribution methods meant that it is both available and reliable for home gardeners; individual systems can now be purchased to combat aphids, mealybugs, red spider mite, scale, sciarid flies, slugs, thrips, vine weevil and whitefly, among other problems. Not all are equally reliable, most are relatively expensive, all need careful application and optimum conditions to work. But when they are good, they are very good and for several years I have neither used nor needed any other treatment against glasshouse whitefly because the biological control agent, the South American wasp-like insect *Encarsia formosa*, is now well established in my propagating house and is self-perpetuating.

CROP ROTATION

Rotation is a technique known to every vegetable gardener, but one that is always done with almost no thought about how realistic or valuable it really is. The principle is simple – ensure the greatest possible time interval between successive crops of the same type of plant on the same area of soil and the differing nutrient requirements of each will ensure that the whole range of soil chemicals is used to the full.

This is probably fair, as is the fact that different crops require different types of soil cultivation and so the whole depth of the soil is properly tilled. But the greatest value of rotation comes, so we are told, from the fact that many pests and diseases are fairly specific in their plant hosts so the populations of these organisms in the soil should die away between crops. This might be the case in commercial fields, where the crops are physically far apart, but it really makes little sense in the home kitchen garden. I say this first because many garden pests and diseases aren't specific to

particular plants; the grey mould fungus (*Botrytis cinerea*) and the potato-peach aphid (*Myzus persicae*), for instance, both affect a wide range of species. Secondly, some of the most significant problems (club root on brassicas and white rot on onions, for example) will certainly not die away in the three seasons between rotations but can survive unaided for twenty or more years. Moreover, in a garden or allotment the distance between plots is likely to be a few metres at the most. The rotation principle takes no account of the fact that many pests can fly or even that soil contaminated with disease organisms will be moved on spades, wheelbarrows and gardeners' boots. Crop rotation is sound enough in theory but its benefits in gardens will be almost entirely nutritional.

LEFT: Seeing white fly scales on tomato leaves turn black is encouraging evidence that they have been parasitized by Encarsia formosa. *ABOVE: Potato blight spores persist for a very short time in the soil, so rotation is of no benefit.*

TREE AND SHRUB
GARDENING

TREE AND SHRUB GARDENING

Trees, gardens and people have collectively had a bad press in the UK recently and tree planting is probably the only area of gardening in recent times about which the government has considered legislating. Admittedly, most of the blame can be laid squarely at the base of one species, or to be more correct, one hybrid: the Leyland cypress (x *Cupressocyparis leylandii*) or, to be even more correct, at the feet of public ignorance about tree biology in general and about the biology of this plant in particular. Behind this situation lies much that is relevant to trees, shrubs, hedges and gardening, and the absence of common sense that has pervaded the whole.

The background to the legislative saga is most simply summarized in the opening paragraph of a British government Research Paper published in 2001: 'The issue of high hedges has received extensive publicity as rapid growth evergreen hedges have become increasingly popular over the last 30 years as a way of screening neighbouring properties from each other.' Anyone who might have doubted how well informed the authorities really were about trees and hedges had their suspicions confirmed in the next sentence: 'The species most frequently of concern is the Leyland Cyprus [*sic*].' The document proceeded to tell us that not only was the 'Leyland Cyprus' a problem, but also that Lawson cypress, thuja, privet, yew and holly had 'similar characteristics'. Really? Annual growth rates and ultimate heights were quoted for them, although in almost all instances, the measurements given were at some variance from my own experiences.

I don't for a moment deny the fact that trees and hedges constitute problems in some gardens, both to the owners and to their neighbours, but the several attempts to control the matter by legislation have failed at an early hurdle. The Control of Residential Hedgerows Bill (1998/1999) didn't reach a second reading. The Statutory Nuisances (Hedgerows in Residential Areas) Bill (1999/2000) did reach report stage in the House of Lords but then failed to progress further, while the Private Member's High Hedges Bill (2000/2001), despite government support, failed to complete all its stages of scrutiny before the 2001 general election and so also did not become law.

Sooner or later no doubt, legislation along the lines of the High Hedges Bill will reach the statute book in Britain and elsewhere but I wonder how much difference it will make. Its main provisions were 'for local authorities . . . to determine complaints by the owners/occupiers of residential property affected by evergreen hedges that are over 2 metres [7 feet] high and obstruct light to the complainant's home or garden'. Requiring people who already have high hedges or trees to do something about them is only a minor part of the subject. Much more important is the education of

Topiary offers a most attractive way of growing garden trees – but your enthusiasm must be kept within bounds.

Big trees can cause problems – both while they are growing and when they blow over.

the public about the best choice of trees and hedging plants for particular situations and how to look after them so the problem of unacceptably high hedges doesn't arise. And it is here that the singling out of the Leyland cypress becomes particularly apposite. It is certainly an inappropriate tree for urban gardens. That notable tree expert, the late Alan Mitchell wrote in 1985, 'Unless wholesale tipping and clipping starts very soon, all these areas will in 40 years be under dense forest 30 metres [100 feet] tall'. But that is the urban situation. I know of gardens in exposed rural localities that simply couldn't exist had a windbreak of this tree not been planted initially to enable other trees and shrubs to establish. Then, when it had fulfilled its purpose, it had been cut down.

In taking the commonsense approach to the subject, I shall look at trees, shrubs and hedges separately because the considerations for each aren't the same, but first I ought to try and define the differences between the three. And I shall have to invent these as there is nothing universally accepted and in any event they are defined on the basis of the way they have been grown, not on what species they are. For my present purposes, a tree is a woody plant that naturally attains a height of more than 6m/20ft on a single stem; a shrub is a woody plant, usually with many stems, that doesn't. A hedge is a collection of woody plants, trees or shrubs, planted close together in a line and managed in a more or less identical fashion.

CHOOSING TREES

I am sure that more problems are caused through gardeners using trees incorrectly or inappropriately than in any other aspect of gardening – less common sense is used than almost anywhere else. Quite simply, the reason is that trees are big – by my definition, the smallest will ultimately be 6m/20ft tall – and any mistakes made in the choice of species or variety and of planting position will therefore be magnified. Leaving aside the small minority of gardeners who have space to plant copses or even woods, a tree is a specimen feature. And in most modern gardens the overall space available dictates that it be a solitary and therefore important specimen feature. This being so, the tree for the modern gardener has an exacting list of attributes to satisfy. It must be of a size and shape commensurate with the scale of the garden so that visually it is correct. It must also be of a size and habit that will not dominate the space around it to the extent of adversely affecting the growth of other plants. Its size and growth habit must not be such that it poses a threat to the structure of the house or other buildings. Moreover, it must appear attractive for as much of the year as possible – you can't hide a dull tree or move it out of the way as the glory of its leaves or blossom fades. And it mustn't for any of these reasons offend the neighbours.

Planting a tree in a garden simply because you like the look of it and then cutting it down if it happens to grow larger than you wish is the wrong way to go about things. It can also lead you into serious practical complications because in some areas (such as statutory Conservation Areas in England and Wales) there are legal impediments to the felling of trees once they have exceeded a certain size. Just because you put it there, you aren't necessarily entitled to remove it. But what size is appropriate for your garden, how do you allow for the fact that trees grow bigger year by year and what do you do while you wait for them to fill the allotted space?

In considering what size of tree to choose (ultimate size that is), try to relate it to garden area and the height of the house or other buildings. Remember that to be effective in obscuring some distant unsightly object, a tree doesn't need to be so large as to mask it completely. Simply breaking the skyline is often perfectly adequate and a

narrow tree can therefore achieve a result you may have imagined needed something wide-spreading.

Work on the old guideline that a tree's roots spread as far below ground as its branches do above and you will have a reasonable indication of the likely effect on nearby vegetation. Look at the density of the canopy – see how close the branches are together and (if you are buying or choosing in the growing season) how large and numerous the leaves and you will be able to judge how much light penetrates to ground level. Self-evidently, a tree with a mass of tiny branches and either many small leaves or fewer large ones will cast the densest shade and have the greatest impact on what grows beneath. And if your tree is deciduous, look at your reference books to discover whether it is late or early coming into leaf or flushing, and late or early in losing its foliage in autumn. This information isn't always readily available but it can be important. A tree that flushes late in the spring will have little impact on early flowering plants, especially bulbs, that are growing beneath, as they will be in bloom at a time when light can still reach down to soil level.

When choosing how big a tree you want and the characteristics it must have, the best advice I can give is to look in as many authoritative reference books as possible. Check, double check and triple check its ultimate size and growth rate. You should certainly not rely on the label attached to the plant at the garden centre. I have

yet to meet anyone who will own up to writing these labels, but the information is at best vague, sometimes misleading, sometimes totally wrong. They usually originate in Holland, Italy or other places where the trees were grown (and usually grown extremely well; there's nothing much wrong with European nursery stock) but they do seem to lose a great deal in translation.

Weeping willows are plants for lake-sides and large parks – the amount of water they withdraw from the soil can create problems for nearby buildings.

It is impossible to give general advice on the planting of trees such that they will present no hazard to any building under any circumstances, but one rule of thumb I employ is never to plant weeping willows or the more vigorous poplars in anything other than a large garden. Another is never to plant any tree closer to a house than one and a half times its ultimate height. I have been accused in the past of being too cautious in this advice and I concede that it does exclude from many gardens trees that could be relatively harmless but when you are starting afresh, it is wise to be careful. Nonetheless, I have no wish to cause alarm to those many gardeners who already have trees much closer than this to their houses (as I do myself). If you are in doubt about existing trees, do seek expert guidance – experienced, qualified and properly insured tree surgeons operate in all areas.

The impact of any tree on a building is dependent on a number of factors; it isn't simply a matter of the roots growing into the brickwork and damaging it directly. There are other indirect effects mediated through the soil and the first factor is the species itself: its growth rate and its water demand (the amount of water that it removes from the soil). The water demand is high for a weeping willow or poplar, which is why I single them out, but low for a magnolia or wisteria, which is why they are safely trained against countless house walls. The second factor is the soil type, the effect of any tree being greater on heavy clays than on light, free draining sands because when roots extract moisture from the soil they cause clay to shrink in dry conditions, only to swell again in wet weather. The depth of the building's foundations and the local climate (rainfall and evaporation rates are particularly significant) are additional factors. Conversely, it is no use imagining that an existing situation will necessarily be solved by felling a suspect tree because its removal will take away a large water pump with the possible consequence that the soil will become saturated and so begin to heave. Remember the statistic that on a warm day, one square metre of leaf cover will lose over 5 litres of water. And even the severing of major roots without removal of the tree can give rise to soil swelling on some sites. Because of the complexity of the matter therefore, my strong advice is always to engage a competent expert before taking any action over a tree that is causing concern because of its size and position.

Having a tree of the correct size is only part of the story. It must not possess other antisocial features such as large quantities of enormous leaves that block all around them when they fall; nor must it be prone to infestation by aphids and so give rise to sticky honeydew that cascades over people, cars and other vegetation. The most important of the positive attributes is that the tree should have all year round appeal – for after all, when it is alone or at best, one of a small number, a tree really must earn its keep.

The most obviously attractive parts of a tree are its leaves but you should bear in mind the length of time they are present to be admired. Evergreens bear leaves all year round (although contrary to what is sometimes imagined, they do still shed them – they simply do it piecemeal) and on that score might be thought to offer the best value. Unfortunately, they tend to retain them monotonously and unchanging. Deciduous trees generally have more attractive leaves than evergreens although a deciduous species that comes into leaf late and sheds its foliage early is scarcely offering you much value. Nonetheless, the foliage of many deciduous trees changes colour (and in a few instances, shape) as the season progresses. One that offers changing leaf interest therefore is especially to be cherished and once the leaves have fallen from a deciduous tree in autumn, much of interest and attractiveness may still remain in the shape of the twigs, bark and buds. Although there are rather few trees worth growing for these attributes alone, the following three are all in my garden, all originate from the same part of the world and are probably among the best:

Acer grosseri var. *hersii*

The Chinese snake-bark maple is, I think, the loveliest of all the snake-barks. The bark is vertically streaked in an olive green snakeskin pattern that contrasts beautifully with the pink tinge of the young shoots. It is also (or at least mine is), a particularly graceful tree, arching outwards from almost fastigiate lower branches to form a vase shape with drooping shoot tips.

Betula utilis var. jacquemontii

The West Himalayan birch is arguably the best of the white-barked Himalayan birches, which are a confusingly uniform group. The beautiful white bark peels away like paper to reveal a new softly pink layer beneath. They don't seem to be as seriously plagued by aphids as our native birches, and often divide below soil level, giving rise to more than one trunk. This is an effect that people often try to emulate with birches in general by planting small groups of trees close together. I inherited a superb fairly mature, twin-trunked specimen with the garden but do be aware that these are ultimately rather large trees. Mine, about forty years old at a guess, is now around 12m/40ft high and across, and still growing vigorously.

Prunus serrula

The birch-bark tree from Western China, often called the Tibetan cherry, has the bark that people can't resist touching with the result that the lower parts of the trunk, within reach, are like burnished cooper. In truth, without regular 'polishing' the bark becomes rather dark and dull.

Almost all trees also bear flowers (collectively called blossom when they are present in large numbers), and many trees are chosen for their blossom alone. Nonetheless, many trees and shrubs (like lilacs or

ABOVE: The bark of Acer grosseri *var.* hersii.
BELOW: The fruits of Sorbus aucucuparia.

Japanese flowering cherries) that are selected for a stunning floral display then offer a fairly depressing spectacle for all of the months after the blossom has fallen and I seldom use a tree in a small garden that has blossom as its major feature. Flowers are followed by fruit, the colour or shape of which may also be attractive. But the period over which fruit can contribute to the appeal of a garden tree is generally limited by the local bird population who will view it, quite understandably, as a free and convenient food supply.

PLANTING AND CULTIVATION

As with all other plants, good trees begin with good planting although the possibility that you are putting something in place for a lifetime does magnify its importance. The traditional time for planting trees is during the dormant season from late autumn until early spring but this is only really relevant for bare-rooted plants. Most of the trees that are now supplied through garden centres are in containers and these can be planted at all times of the year, although establishment will still generally be more sure during the dormant period. I cannot over-emphasize the importance of giving thorough and careful preparation to the planting position. Dig a hole of volume approximately twice that of the root ball of the

I've always taken the view that teasing away the outer roots of a container-grown plant will encourage growth outwards rather than inwards.

tree and pile the soil at the side. Then mix with this a similar volume of well-rotted manure or garden compost and several handfuls of bone meal. Break up the soil in the base of the hole with a fork then gradually refill, pressing it down gently with your boot until the remaining hole is deep enough for the tree's roots to be spread out in it while leaving the original soil mark on the trunk level with the soil surface.

With container-grown plants, many gardeners, including some good gardeners, simply place the whole ball of compost into the planting hole and refill. I have always taken the view that establishment is better if some of the roots around the sides and bottom of the compost ball are

gently teased out first. This gives them encouragement to grow outwards into the soil and not simply turn back inwards to the cosy and moist environment in which they have previously been growing. Then insert a stout stake on the leeward side of the tree (to ensure that it is blown away from, and not on to it). Although short stakes have become rather popular, working on the principle that the more its stem flexes, the stronger a tree will become, I'm not convinced and there are graphic examples of their ineffectiveness in some young street trees in my own village, which are permanently arched over like an old English long bow. I prefer a purpose cut stake of approximately 1.5m/5ft, made of treated timber, and driven at least 60cm/24in into the ground. The tree's trunk should be secured to the stake with two belt-style tree ties, one close to the top and one close to ground level. Then the hole should gradually be filled in around the roots with the soil and organic matter mixture, the plant moved up and down to remove air pockets, then pressed down gently with your boot. The area around the plant must be watered thoroughly, then finally, a small mound of manure or compost made around the base of the trunk to ensure water doesn't puddle.

Because trees ultimately grow large there is a tendency to think of them as self-sufficient. In practice, in the early years they require as much feeding, watering, mulching and protection from competition with weeds as shrubs and herbaceous perennials do. It is particularly important therefore not to allow grass or other vegetation to grow up to the stem base. Where young trees are planted in lawns moreover, a circle of turf, approximately 1m/3¼ft in diameter, should be removed from around the trunk. Fertilizer and organic mulch should then be applied to this area. Small trees (those up to about 5m/16ft in height) may be grown in containers of soil-based John Innes No. 3 potting compost; a container of 75–100cm/2½–3¼ft in diameter will be needed. It should be remembered that the tree will require considerable attention to watering during the summer but among those I consider especially suitable for containers are fruit trees on dwarfing rootstocks, the smaller types of Japanese cherry, Japanese maple, hawthorn, laurel and magnolia.

HEDGES

Although some species of tree and shrub are seen in gardens more commonly as hedges than as free-standing plants, there is nothing intrinsically different about the species that are grown in this way. They need only one important attribute but several others are desirable and make the difference between a successful hedge and an unsuccessful one. By definition, hedges are retained at a certain size and in a certain shape by clipping. Their principal attribute must therefore be the ability to respond to clipping, by which I mean the possession of a dense, twiggy form and a large number of lateral buds that will burst in life on each shoot when the terminal buds are clipped away.

This is true of all 'conventional' foliage hedges, whether evergreen like cypresses, yew and holly or deciduous like beech. Among the additional desirable attributes are the absence of the pest and disease problems like aphids and mildew that so commonly affect plants with a dense, close habit, a resistance to honey fungus, total frost hardiness and a root system that doesn't impoverish the soil over a considerable area.

All hedges satisfy some of the most important criteria for an efficient wind screen – they are pliable and they are at least partly permeable. The forest tree and commercial fruit growing industries have carried out considerable research into methods of protecting plants against the effects of strong wind and two main facts have emerged. The first is that the most effective means of lessening the damage from strong winds is with a barrier that is fifty per cent permeable, in other

We are generally too conservative with our hedging plants – mix species together for added interest.

words, one that only obstructs 50 per cent of the wind – it is half solid and half holes. It might at first seem that the more complete the barrier, the greater would be its value but a totally solid obstruction like a garden wall has two drawbacks. Firstly, the full face it presents renders it quite likely to be damaged itself, and secondly, it serves merely to deflect the wind upwards. This causes a low pressure area on the leeward side with consequent down currents and eddies that, at worst, may be as damaging as the original wind and, at best, may cause countless leaves or crisp packets (depending on the neighbourhood in which you live), to accumulate in your garden.

The second important fact that emerged from research on windbreaks is that they are effective for a distance on the leeward side of around thirty times their heights although the maximum benefit extends for only about ten times. So, the standard 2m/6½ft garden boundary hedge will effectively provide protection from the wind for about 20m/65ft; adequate therefore for the width of most gardens. Because of the regular trimming that you give to hedges, their height is also low in relation to the extent and depth of their root systems. So even in the strongest of gales, hedges are almost never damaged. Another desirable hedge attribute is relatively rapid growth – watching a hedge take twenty years before it achieves even the most basic of its required purposes is no pleasurable pastime. Nor should it grow too rapidly, however. It may be regrettable but it is an unavoidable

feature of fast-growing plants that they don't stop when they have reached your chosen height. They keep on growing and lead to exactly the problems associated with Leyland cypress I mentioned earlier.

My own solution to the need for privacy, shelter and protection during the six or eight years while your young hedge grows is to plant it alongside an attractive fence which will itself be coming towards the end of its useful life as the hedge begins its own. Hurdles of interwoven willow are ideal because they are fairly flexible and most importantly have sufficient permeability (plenty of small holes) to avoid damage by even really strong winds. I have used a large number of willow hurdles over the years but find they vary considerably in their life expectancy. Partly this is understandable, due to the position in which they are used – those more fully exposed last for about

I have made extensive use of willow hurdles to provide screening and protection while my yew hedges grow.

seven years; those more protected almost twice that. But durability and robustness also vary enormously between manufacturers and, so the manufacturers themselves tell me, with the quality and age of the willow withies and, rather satisfyingly, with the skill of the man who made the hurdle. My advice therefore is to buy from a specialist hurdle maker, tell him about your precise needs, choose willow rather than hazel, which I find not nearly as durable, practical or attractive in gardens, and be prepared to pay for wonderful age-old craftsmanship.

Hedges with a dense, foliar habit are generally planted in the garden as boundaries, affording privacy, wind protection and a visual backdrop to other garden features. Used in this way, they extend the life of the garden up to its limits and have a softness that no artificial barrier ever will. They also harbour wildlife, providing nesting and roosting places for birds, and shelter and homes for small mammals and countless types of insect. This is of course, a double-edged attribute, as not all the wildlife resident in the hedge is beneficial to the rest of the garden. Pest species are also given shelter and winter quarters there and a hedge can be a haven from which invasive weeds like ground elder and bindweed march outwards at regular intervals. Nonetheless, this is a small price to pay for helping preserve an example of at least a few metres of one of the most fascinating of habitats, and one that has disappeared over vast areas of commercial farmland.

It makes much sense therefore to use foliage hedges as boundaries but it is often overlooked that they can have other uses, equally important, within the body of the garden as structural features of many kinds. I use evergreen hedges ranging in size from 15cm/6in to 3m/10ft tall for dividing the garden into discrete areas, as the edging to beds, borders and more formal features such as knot gardens (which are themselves of course dependent for their appearance on exactly the same types of hedging), herb and kitchen gardens and as isolated features – when they are generally referred to as topiary. Topiary is under-used in gardens and can play an interesting and valuable role in designs of many types, not simply the formal plantings with which it is generally associated.

Buying hedging plants can be an expensive hobby, especially if you obtain them from your garden centre in containers. It makes much more sense to buy them bare-rooted in bundles from a forest tree nursery at a fraction of the cost. And much the best way of planting them is to prepare a trench, rather than individual planting holes, with thorough digging and generous applications of organic matter and bone meal. The difference in the growth and appearance between a hedge which has been planted in really well-prepared soil and one which has simply been stuck into the ground with little care can be staggering; and of course it is legacy that will be with you, prominently, for a long time. I always space

hedging plants about 25 per cent closer together than many people recommend because I want an effect as quickly as possible. The increased competition brought about by closer spacing is in my experience only significant in the early years and is easily countered by feeding the hedge with a general fertilizer every spring, and mulching it too. For a wide hedge (more than about 45cm/18in), it is worth planting in two or even three rows with the individual plants offset from each other. With low or dwarf hedges, I really do pack the plants in closely. The box plants in my knot garden were as close together as I could crowd them – about 5cm/2in apart rather than the 10–20cm/1–8in which is generally recommended. The result was that I had an attractive knot garden within two years rather than waiting an eternity for the gaps between the plants to close and the bare soil to disappear.

By planting the box close together, my knot garden appeared attractive within the first two seasons.

I was fortunate to have a knot garden of any sort, as I was competing with Hampton Court Palace. I planted my knot garden in 1994–5, when the magnificent Privy Garden at Hampton Court was being restored to its early-eighteenth-century glory, vast lines of dwarf box hedging included. I couldn't obtain box for love or money and was told that the Hampton Court project had cleared out most of the nurseries of western Europe. Whether this was true or not, I considered myself extremely fortunate to find a private gardener with a passion for propagation and who had several thousand box plants surplus to his own requirements. I pounced.

After planting a new hedge, don't wait until the plants have attained the desired ultimate height before you start to cut or you will have lush growth towards the top and bareness towards the base – a line of small trees rather than a proper hedge. Trim them each year from the first season after planting, (cutting away approximately one third of the previous season's growth) to encourage bushiness. And similarly, trim the sides too.

One of the odder garden features that comes and goes in popularity is the flowering hedge – the hedge composed of flowering rather than essentially foliage shrubs. Hedges are supposed to be clipped but, unlike a foliage hedge, clipping a flowering hedge diminishes rather than enhances its effect and encourages leaves at the expense of flowers. It is a situation appropriately described in a phrase I treasure, which I once heard a politician say in relation to something quite different: 'Of course you will still get more; you will simply get less more.' Snipping away flowers or flower buds might stimulate a few flower buds to break from further down each shoot, but it will be poor reward for those you have removed. A flowering hedge should only be clipped therefore after one season's flowers have faded and before the following season's buds have formed. This 'window of opportunity' may not be very long and it will usually give you the chance of only one cut each year. By its nature, therefore, a flowering hedge is a much more loose, open structured thing than a conventional foliage hedge. And for this reason, unless the whole is allowed to grow tall and wide, it may simply not be dense enough to function effectively as a garden boundary and is better as an internal garden feature.

SHRUBS

The most important part of my distinction between shrubs and trees is not their ultimate size (although few shrubs are much taller than 6m/20ft), but the fact that most shrubs are multi-stemmed. Nonetheless, like trees, they range greatly in ultimate size and in habit from prostrate, almost two-dimensional plants that spread in all directions except upwards, to vast plants like the *Philadelphus coronarius* at the corner of my kitchen garden, certainly over 6m/20ft tall and with about fifty separate stems. Self-evidently, the

ways in which plants as varied as these can and should be used in the garden are innumerable and for many years I've been saying that the shrub is the most important type of plant in the modern garden. And in this respect, the modern garden is very different from that of a century or more ago. Then, the shrubbery was often a monotonous and rather sombre place, dominated by tough evergreens that assumed their value in the nineteenth-century urban environment because of their tolerance of the atmospheric pollution that accompanied the years following the Industrial Revolution. Colour in those gardens was provided by herbaceous plants or by roses. Today, the shortcomings in this type of reliance have been widely recognized and the dedicated shrubbery is now to be found only in larger gardens.

The modern shrub has other roles. It is at its most valuable when used to provide the permanent framework for a mixed border, where it supplies interest and attractiveness all year round, most importantly in the winter when the herbaceous perennials, bulbs and annuals have died down. But shrubs can also be used most valuably as individual specimens or small groups among other types of plant or in grass. And the

ABOVE: Cornus capitata *is a magnificent flowering shrub with appealing cream white bracts.*
BELOW: My magnificent old Philadelphus coronarius *is technically a shrub, despite being over 6 metres tall.*

interest and appeal they supply can take many forms: massed blossom or striking individual flowers, perfume, attractive bark colour or texture, leaf colour and shape or simply the overall form and shape.

When planning a mixed planting, decide on the shrubs (and trees if they are also to be included) before selecting the herbaceous perennials and use a mixture of evergreen and deciduous types. As it is hardest to obtain reliable colour and interest in the border in late autumn to early winter, begin by choosing shrubs with variegated evergreen foliage or attractive fruits. Place these at the back of the border (or in the centre of an island

ABOVE: I've never liked island beds – of any size. They look like horticultural lost souls. RIGHT: One of my favourite shrubs, the Chilean Crinodendron hookerianum, *makes a superb specimen but sadly my own soil is not sufficiently acidic for it.*

bed if you like such things – to me they always look like lost souls, wandering the garden in search of a proper home). In the middle of the border, choose shrubs that offer flowering or foliage interest in spring and summer or perhaps a variegated holly or other evergreen trained in a standard or column shape. Shrubs for the front of the border must be neat, particularly where the edge of the border meets the lawn and evergreen types such as small hebes or lavenders are invaluable here. In a shallow border, growing a shrub such as a pyracantha trained two-dimensionally against the back wall will economize on space but you should remember to allow access for pruning.

A shrubbery tends to be less interesting year-round than a mixed border but it has a place in large gardens where maintenance of perennials is a problem. To increase its appeal, consider incorporating scented, winter-flowering shrubs like *Chimonanthus praecox*, *Sarcococca* or a *Viburnum* that can be used for cutting. When creating a shrub border, you will find that adherence to the correct planting distance will leave large gaps in the early years but don't be tempted to plant closer than recommended or your plants will soon suffer through the increased competition. It is much better to mulch well between the plants and to use inexpensive short-term perennials or even annuals to fill the gaps, gradually taking them out, or planting fewer each year, until the shrubs reach maturity.

Small, tough evergreen shrubs with good leaf cover can be used as a ground-cover. This may not be the most exciting way of planting and I'm the first to admit that the invention of the 'ground-cover' has been one of the saddest facets of twentieth century gardening. No plant that is chosen purely for its function as a space-filler is ever likely to be enhancing the appeal of your garden a great deal, but it does offer a way of

dealing with a potentially difficult area such as a shady slope.

There is no compulsion about growing shrubs in borders, however, and those with outstanding beauty or form make fine isolated specimens. If it is impact from flowers that you are seeking, then look no further than *Camellia*, *Magnolia*, *Philadelphus*, *Syringa* or *Paeonia*; but always be aware of my caveats about boredom for the rest of the year and the drawback of relying on the spectacular flowers of a specimen that is vulnerable to weather damage – late frosts on

Rhododendron yakushimanum *is a wonderful small species appropriate for container growing.*

spring flowers and heavy rain on summer flowers. The alternative is to rely on the more weather-tolerant and generally longer lasting appeal that derives from particularly fine foliage or overall shape. Here, the Oriental species of *Acer*, *Cornus kousa* and its relatives, *Cotinus coggygria*, *Fothergilla*, *Liquidambar* and *Sambucus*, among others, are well worth considering. Although foliage is generally more tolerant of adverse weather than flowers are, do be aware nonetheless that cold winds and exposed sites will be to the detriment of some golden- and variegated-leaved forms especially.

Even the smallest garden has room for a few shrubs in containers. To be suitable for container growing, a shrub must be able to tolerate both the restriction of its roots and some periodic drying out. Container growing always offers you the opportunity to grow plants that are intolerant of the natural soil conditions in your garden and, in the case of shrubs, this is particularly useful as there are just so many fine species and varieties that require acidic conditions, and a few similarly desiring of an alkaline environment. Simply by selecting an appropriate compost, you can have the best of both worlds.

Among the more attractive acid-loving shrubs are heathers, for small containers, while compact varieties of *Camellia*, *Pieris*, *Rhododendron* (and *Azalea*) make excellent single subjects for larger pots. Other, less demanding shrubs that adapt well to containers are *Daphne*, among which

some varieties, together with those of *Hamamelis*, have appealing early-season flowers and fragrance. Evergreen shrubs are particularly valuable: in the winter they may provide the main colour on a terrace while in the summer they are an excellent foil for flowering plants. Among those I have found most amenable to containers are *Aucuba*, which is both attractive and tolerant of difficult conditions, and *Buxus*, which of course is a fine topiary subject, readily clipped into appealing shapes. Containers that are light or mobile enough to be transported under cover over the winter allow you to grow shrubs like *Abutilon* and *Callistemon* that are of borderline hardiness.

I want finally to turn my attention to a type of shrub, or rather a way of growing shrubs, that is perhaps the least appreciated – wall shrubs. A wall shrub is any shrub that will grow well when planted close to a wall. This may be because it has a spreading habit that can readily be trained in two dimensions or it may be because it needs the shelter from the wind and cold that only a wall can provide. Some wall shrubs will naturally spread to cover a wall with very little need for training whereas others will require constant and regular attention if they are really to give of their best. They provide a welcome and sensible change from climbers because far too many climbers are in the wrong place. They may have beautiful flowers or even beautiful foliage (although few non-clinging climbers do) but they also have an unkempt, untidy growth that reflects

their natural habit of growing over and cascading from trees or rocks. Trying by pruning and training to turn them into something neat and tidy to clothe your house wall is a thankless and fruitless exercise. How much better to choose a climber with far less pliable stems and a less vigorous growth rate; but forget about calling it a climber and call it a wall shrub instead. After all,

Walls offer a superb and neglected habitat for growing shrubs.

a climber is only a shrub with floppy stems that must have some means of support without which they would slump into a tangled heap. Wall shrubs may sometimes appear better when pegged or tied against a wall in order to keep them neat and tidy but they will stand perfectly well freely without.

To make a good wall shrub, a plant must have a root system that will not cause damage to the fabric or foundations of the wall itself and, by and large, wall shrubs will also function better if they are reasonably tolerant of the dry and perhaps even impoverished soil that is present close to the base of a wall. It is also a great help is they are fairly tolerant of aphids and mildew, the pest and disease problems that are so common in a warm, sheltered wall environment.

Perhaps the commonest and, in many ways, the most successful of wall shrub genera is *Pyracantha*. There really are few plants happier against a wall although it is important to select varieties that are most readily trained in two dimensions. I have spent seasons trying to force pyracanthas that are naturally spreading into upright geometric shapes. My favourite red berried variety is now 'Teton' which really is amenable to being pruned into the most attractive two-dimensional forms.

Another classic wall shrub that brightens up gardens everywhere in the spring is the ornamental Japanese quince, *Chaenomeles*. Its lovely flowers in shades of red and orange as well

as white are followed by the familiar quince fruits although these are not as appealingly edible as true quinces. But here again, choose your varieties with care; 'Spitfire' is a superbly upright red-flowered form.

A large number of shrubs will grow very well against a wall and will benefit from the additional

*The ornamental Japanese quince (*Chaenomeles*) is a fine wall shrub – although some varieties are naturally more two-dimensional than others.*

warmth and protection that the wall offers. Such plants as *Carpenteria, Ceanothus, Ribes speciosum* and many other choice species can be grown in this way in gardens where they would be unlikely to survive in more exposed locations. Do bear in mind, however, that any wall shrub will benefit from particular care being taken over soil preparation and from extra attention being given to feeding and watering. This is because the conditions at the base of a wall can often be dry and impoverished.

KITCHEN GARDENING

KITCHEN GARDENING

In the 1970s and 1980s, when I was involved in horticultural research, we used to quote the figure (accurately, I think) that around one third of British fruit and vegetables were grown in home gardens. I'm told it is now probably slightly under 10 per cent but, despite being a lower proportion, it is a statistic that matters greatly to the people who grow them. Many of us need only go back half a century to our childhoods and the habits instilled by the Dig for Victory campaign of the Second World War to see where the foundations of modern kitchen gardening were laid. Back then, it was the shortage of supplies in the shops and a drive for self-sufficiency that was the impetus. Today, supermarkets are hardly short of produce but the realization that home-grown crops generally do taste better, certainly give you a wider choice of varieties and can be grown under exactly the conditions you choose, has been no less important a motivation.

Oddly enough, it was, in an indirect way, the Second World War that had a curious influence on my own style of kitchen gardening. As a boy, I was always slightly mystified by the way my father, who had arrived in Britain from Poland in 1940, grew his crops. There seemed to be an indiscriminate mixture of vegetables and flowers, unlike the gardens of my friends' fathers who rigidly kept the

The mixture of flowers and vegetables in a traditional Polish allotment was where my father gained the inspiration that later influenced me.

two apart. In those days, for most people, the vegetable plot was something to be secreted away from the gaze of decent folk.

It wasn't until I first visited Poland myself many years later that the explanation became apparent. Living in Warsaw, my father had done as other Polish city-dwellers did. His vegetables had been grown in ogródki działkowé – small gardens grouped together at the edge of the city. Unlike a typical British allotment site, the groups of Polish gardens are very appealing places where the family would be quite likely to spend the weekend. Most are equipped with a small but attractive structure like a small summerhouse. And the flowers and vegetables grow together in a wonderful mélange of colour and fragrance. Today of course, mixed planting has become a fairly widely accepted practice in Britain but forty years ago, it was highly novel. And every year, in every kitchen garden of mine, flowers have been an important feature; and my kitchen garden isn't hidden in some far-flung corner but close to the house where it both looks attractive and is within easy reach of the kitchen.

VEGETABLES

Where space is limited, and that is the case in almost every home garden today, the enthusiasm to grow at least of your some of your own produce must be tempered by some careful thought. You will have insufficient room to grow all you need; even a standard allotment of around 250m²/

300 square yards will barely accommodate everything. Keep in mind that each person in Britain consumes on average over 2.5kg/5½lb of fruit and vegetables per week – over half a tonne a year for a family of four, for which you would need a rather substantial kitchen garden. So unless you are utterly besotted with one particular vegetable, I would advise a median course, carefully selecting the crops to grow, emphasizing some and rejecting some completely. How do you make this choice? There are several ways of approaching the dilemma and the most obvious are to restrict yourself to those that occupy the least space per plant or per crop, to those crops that are the most satisfying, challenging or rewarding to grow, those that are the most expensive to buy in the shops, or those that, for whatever reason, are immeasurably better which picked or cut fresh. Freshness simply cannot be overlooked when considering flavour and it is a fact that many crop plants begin to change chemically as soon as they are taken from the ground.

I can't, and nor would I wish to advise you on your tastes; even if I followed conventional wisdom and tried, I would trip up. Twenty years ago, I might have suggested that swedes would never be likely to feature, many people lumping them, as my father-in-law was wont, with cattle fodder. Then came the likes of the chef Gary Rhodes and the British kitchen revolution, and swede (quite rightly) was on the menu at the smartest London restaurants. But I can offer some guidelines that I hope will help as, like almost everyone else, I too garden with limited space.

You can follow my own practice and grow a little of almost everything; but then I have good reason for wanting to do so. I need to keep my hand in with all types of crops, to sample new varieties and to be able to demonstrate everything, when required, to television viewers. This means that we are self-sufficient for much of the year (allowing for the benefits of the freezer) in soft fruit, tree fruit and some vegetables, including potatoes, onions, carrots and parsnips. We are less self-sufficient, however, in summer crops such as tomatoes and in salads such as lettuce, for a number of reasons.

It is perfectly possible to grow lettuce all year round but it is a fairly thankless task, requiring a considerable input of time and effort, careful planning and, if you include the winter crop, a significant heating bill too. Lettuce is much better as a summer-only venture; and for many years, I have raised the first crops in modules in the propagating house. Direct sowing lettuce in the early part of the season is a chancy business whereas transplants should give you complete success. But once you do begin sowing directly from early summer onwards, don't let yourself in for a glut. Most families are unlikely to want more than one lettuce each day so to spread the season, try sowing a short row of seeds as soon as the seedlings from the previous sowing have emerged; and concentrate on cos and crisp-head

varieties once the weather really warms up. The germination of the seed of most varieties of butterhead (smooth or cabbage) lettuce is suppressed at temperatures above about 25°C/77°F.

From time to time I look at my tomato crop and I find myself asking why I trouble myself with them. For many years, I grew outdoor tomatoes. I embarked with great enthusiasm and tried the latest offerings from the seed companies. I raised the plants with care in the propagating house and planted them out after the danger of frost had passed; and in three years out of five found them laid low a few weeks later by blight. I have never believed that anything can really be done to alleviate the effects of blight on garden tomatoes. The only possibility is a protective spray in anticipation of the conditions being favourable for

I always transplant early lettuces rather than sowing directly – and a spiral arrangement adds interest.

the disease to strike. But adhering to my maxim of refusing to spray anything in the kitchen garden except under the most dire circumstances, I never did anything. The crop was a failure, the space that could have been used for other things was wasted and I still had some fresh tomatoes in the greenhouse where blight is most unlikely. So outdoor tomatoes no longer feature in my plans. But I then ask myself if greenhouse tomatoes make sense either. They don't cost the earth at the supermarket and couldn't the greenhouse space be put to better use? Here, I'm fairly sure the answer is no.

The number of tomato varieties available to gardeners has multiplied in recent years, partly as new commercial hybrids are released to the garden market and partly as old, so-called heritage varieties are rediscovered and promoted. I find most modern tomato varieties fairly tasteless but tomatoes are one of the crops that offer the finest advertisement for growing your own produce. This is simply because you can choose on the single criterion of flavour and select those that might be commercially useless due to maturing at irregular intervals – making harvesting labour intensive and costly – producing too small a crop too slowly, having thin skins – therefore being prone to damage in the journey between producer and supermarket shelf – and so on. This is not to say that all non-commercial varieties are good, or that heritage tomatoes are necessarily better than modern types. But once in while, a

I grow eight tomato plants by ring culture – in bottomless pots over a gravel bed and watered from below – four down each side. Four are of trusted and tried types that I know will yield well – I have settled of late on two plants of 'Gardeners Delight', one of 'Alicante' and one of 'Super Marmande' or a similar large fruited variety. The remaining four are my experiments and it was among these that I discovered 'Summer Cider', a heritage variety of beefsteak or Marmande type but richly orange in colour, with the texture of a mango and a fine flavour. By chance, I recently read a report in a consumer magazine in which this and most other heritage tomato varieties had been 'tested' and were pretty roundly condemned – which seems to prove no more than that there is no accounting for taste. And as for the propagating house compartment being put to better summer use, I'm not sure it can. The tomatoes occupy the space at a time when the propagation of other plants by both seed and cuttings is at a low ebb and there aren't any other temporary plants that would confer greater advantage or benefits. So greenhouse tomatoes remain.

revelation arises which makes all the experimentation and all the varieties that prove disappointing worthwhile. The outer compartment of my propagating house is given over to tomatoes every summer. Once half-hardy summer plants have been taken outside at the end of May,

Potatoes take up a great deal of room; but it is room that I never begrudge setting aside because the flavour of the first dug new potatoes each year is matchless. And it is the first dug tubers that matter; even the second digging isn't quite the same. So even if I could only grow one early potato plant, I would still do so. I met a nun once

ABOVE: Ring culture pots of tomatoes take the place of the early season cuttings and seed trays in my propagation house. RIGHT: Heritage tomatoes are too often maligned. Some old varieties, like 'Summer Cider' are splendid.

who did just that and planted one tuber of one early variety in a big bucket on the steps of her caravan. I could empathize with that. I grow five or six early potato varieties each year, currently including 'Lady Balfour', 'Red Duke of York' and the new variety 'Juliette' and I don't mind if I am still digging earlies by October, when by rights maincrop potatoes should be lifted for storage. Early potatoes can be stored just as effectively as later varieties.

Maincrop potatoes are, for me, almost the least rewarding of all plants to grow. Admittedly indispensable for the kitchen, they have none of the appeal of the new/early potato, occupy a considerable amount of space, offer little of a challenge, are never prohibitively expensive in the shops, especially if you buy in bulk – although 'Pink Fir Apple' does still seem to cost the earth – and epitomize the purely functional approach to gardening. Although I grow a few, including my trusted old friend 'King Edward' and 'Pink Fir Apple', overall they come down my list of priorities.

Despite what I have said about the excellence of swedes in the kitchen, they are seldom successful as garden plants for reasons I have never truly been able to fathom. Unless you grow them, as farmers do, not in rows but in large blocks (which of course itself means taking up a

The first digging of the early potatoes is one of the most satisfying moments in my kitchen garden year.

large amount of space), they hardly ever succeed. Their relatives, turnips, offer another frustration. They too are wonderful to eat, at least when young and little bigger than a golf ball, and much easier than swedes to grow successfully (they do respond to being sown in rows). However, they are almost invariably plagued with flea beetle, aphids and mildew. These don't necessarily reduce yield seriously but they make for a dirty, messy plant. If that doesn't deter you, then grow them by all means and choose a well-tried variety like 'Snowball'. The alternative of course is to buy your turnips, flea beetle and mildew-free, from a shop; but unless you can find organically grown turnips, you will be eating a crop that, to be free from this many problems, has inevitably been liberally sprayed.

Staying with the same plant family, the Brassicaceae, which generally tends to give us rather large, rather coarse-looking crops, we come to cabbages and the group of closely related plants that have been derived from them: Brussels spouts, cauliflowers and broccoli. I defer to no one in my enjoyment of them on the plate but, by and large, they aren't plants for limited area. In order to assess their practicality for you, let me simply remind you that most cabbages and cauliflowers are grown at a spacing between plants of about 45cm/18in. It is simple arithmetic to work out that one or at best two meals will take up a substantial slice of soil area. Brussels sprouts are a better bet because you should manage perhaps half a dozen meals per plant. Better still are the cut-and-come-again brassicas, calabrese and broccoli. Calabrese is the relative newcomer, an Italian invention, a fast-maturing broccoli whose heads can be picked in the year it is sown and which has the merit of freezing and keeping extremely well, although those virtues have become for me its undoing and the only reason that I don't grow it is that it has become something of a personal *bête noire*. I have travelled the world from (almost) the poles to the equator and have found that simply because of its durability, calabrese has become the universal restaurant stand-by. It has appeared equally intrusively and incongruously among the subtleties of Japanese cuisine and the exotic ingredients of the Caribbean. I have simply grown sick and tired of its lurid green lumpiness. But purple-sprouting broccoli (or its white derivative) is another matter. It's a biennial, long in the ground (around twelve months from sowing to first picking) and long in our collective national kitchen but one you can continue picking over many weeks. A row of six plants, which I now grow, provides us with plenty enough.

The other common root vegetables belong to different families: carrots and parsnips, along with celery and celeriac are in the Apiaceae, which also embraces parsley and several other herbs. They are plants for almost every kitchen garden. Even if you have room only for a row or two of carrots and beetroot, grow them because the flavour of the fresh young crop surpasses anything your supermarket can provide. There's no need these days even to bother with a succession of early, mid-season and late carrot varieties; nor for the business of either lifting them to store in sand or covering them *in situ* in the ground in the way beloved of an earlier generation of kitchen gardeners. I grow one variety, 'Fly Away', all year round, sowing three times in mid-Spring, early summer and late summer. It is durable enough to survive over winter in Warwickshire, and because of its carrot fly resistance, is seldom affected by this pest except when old and over-mature; and it has a good sweet flavour. Hats off to my old friend Bob Ellis who bred it; his enduring legacy to the kitchen garden. A newer variety, 'Resistafly F1', a maincrop, is said by its suppliers to extend the carrot fly resistant season to twelve months of the year. It is too soon for me to form a judgment on its merits and I can only reiterate that I already achieve this with 'Fly Away'.

Provided you are really careful with sowing, there should be no need to thin carrots; having a range of sizes in the crop as a result of some being a bit closer together causes me no problems. The same isn't true of beetroot because each beetroot 'seed' is really a seed ball comprising a small cluster of individual seeds and if these are all left, they will indeed be too crowded for their own good. My preferred beetroot is still the fairly old variety 'Boltardy' but these too must be pulled when young; at around ten or eleven weeks they will start to be at their best. Beetroots are today among the most neglected of the easy-to-grow vegetable crops but they are truly versatile. Par-boiled and then roasted with beef is perhaps their most splendid fate but served cold in summer salads with a waxy salad potato like 'Charlotte' or as an essential ingredient of some wonderful cold summer or hot winter soups doesn't come far behind. For something even more unexpected, boil and then chop them finely to mix with freshly grated horseradish. And the leaves of the young plants can be used in summer salads.

Spinach is both delicious and problematic. It will grow even on fairly heavy soils but frustration arises on light soils like mine where no amount of organic matter and watering will prevent it from bolting. It's perhaps worth saying something about bolting or running to seed as the whole phenomenon is grotesquely fascinating and has different origins in different types of plant. The commonest cause is that the plants have been exposed to cold temperatures at a certain critical stage of their early growth and nothing, not even prolonged exposure to high temperatures, can reverse this. In Chinese cabbage, another bolt-prone crop, it arises from an inter-relationship between temperature and day-length and is best circumvented by sowing fast-growing varieties after mid-summer. In spinach however, bolting is

Swiss chard is an attractive alternative to spinach on light soils although its flavour is rather different.

almost entirely caused by a check to growth brought about by erratic availability of water. This gives a signal to the plant that its survival, and, in turn, that of its entire species is threatened. As with other living things under such stress, the plants do the only thing possible and reproduce themselves.

No spinach variety succeeds reliably in my garden and that is why I turned to, and came to value, the merits of alternatives. Leaf beet was my first adventure. This is a general name for the various large-leaved chards (Swiss, silver, ruby, rhubarb and so on) which are also known as seakale beet. (To complicate matters further, real seakale isn't a beet but, like real kale, a relative of the brassicas.) The chards are good enough plants and the forms known as rhubarb chard (red stems) and rainbow chard (some red and some yellow stems) are rather pretty things. But they are coarser in texture and flavour than spinach and a better substitute is another plant that, like chard, is

a beetroot relative and is better called leaf beet, or perhaps more helpfully, perennial spinach. This is mild and soft-textured enough to be used exactly like real spinach and wilted in a pan with butter and garlic. It isn't properly perennial and is best treated as a biennial. But it doesn't run to seed; at least not until well into the second season.

I'd rather garden on light than heavy soil and mine is perfect for the pea and bean family, the Fabaceae. This is a group of plants that tend to suffer from root rot and poor germination on heavy sites but on a light soil they have the virtue that they can generally be grown repeatedly on the same area of ground without serious consequences. In practice, they can be left out of rotations. There is mysterious disease called pea and bean decline that I investigated in my research days in the early 1980s. Commercial crops began to show signs of root and stem base decay when they had been grown repeatedly on the same fields, even on light soils, but it isn't something I have ever seen in a garden.

Few modern conveniences have had a greater an impact on kitchen gardening than the frozen pea. Because it was one of the first vegetables to prove itself amenable to large scale commercial production, automated harvesting and quick freezing while still maintaining a tolerably good flavour, it ousted the canned marrowfat pea from grocers' shops and the nation's affections. Sadly, it also meant the garden pea was one of the first vegetables to be abandoned by home gardeners because they were no longer prepared to go to the trouble of sowing the seeds, protecting them from mice and birds, erecting supports and then experiencing what is at best a fairly small yield per unit area and a fairly short cropping season – always with the likelihood that if the timing isn't right, the early crop will be mutilated by pea moth. Having said all of that, it does take a home-grown and home-picked crop to make you realize that, while frozen peas are pretty good, they aren't that good and a few rows really are rewarding. Select from a range of early, mid-season and late varieties, with mange tout and sugar snaps as further options – and learn by experience when is the best time to sow in your area to ensure there will no plants in flower in early or mid-summer when the pea moth lays its eggs; sow earlier or later.

I discard most tenets when I sow peas. Conventional wisdom tells you to rake a shallow hollow about 30cm/12in wide (a rake's width) over the whole sowing area and either scatter the seeds in it or drop them in three rows 10cm/4in apart before raking the soil back again. That's fine if you have plenty of area to play with, but in a space-intensive kitchen garden like mine, I am left with the problem of where to rake the soil heaps. I find in any event that replacing the soil is difficult to do without raking a large number of the seeds to the surface or to one end of the bed. So I simply lay my planting plank (the plank on which I stand to work without trampling the soil) down the centre of my standard 1.2m-/4ft-wide bed and crouch on it,

sowing in three staggered rows either side and pushing the seeds into the ground with my thumb with approximately 5cm/2in spacing between each. I gently rake the surface in order to fill the holes with soil, place 1.5m-/5ft-long bamboo canes in a tent pattern over each side of the bed and tie standard plastic pea netting over them.

I'm still uncertain if autumn sowing of the winter-hardy varieties of broad bean like 'Aquadulce' or 'Aquadulce Claudia' is worthwhile. I did it for many years, religiously placing my glass-and-wire Chase tall barn cloches over them (the only type of cloche worth having). But it is a time-consuming task: the cloches need effective anchoring against the wind and some form of watering (a seeper or sprinkler hose for example)

ABOVE LEFT: I minimize the effects of pea moth by choosing my sowing time to avoid the period when the females are egg-laying. ABOVE RIGHT: Growing broad beans under cloches will advance the growing season – but not, I find, by a great deal.

must be laid and pegged down under them because, by spring, the soil beneath can be dry and hand-watering under a cloche is no game for the faint-hearted. And at the end of the day, I gain at best three weeks maturity over crops grown from seeds sown in the early spring. In colder climates, the difference might be greater and make it worthwhile but I'm now inclining against the practice.

In the past I have written something along the lines of: 'The French can keep their French beans; they simply provide a stop-gap until real beans (runners) mature.' On reflection, that might have been slightly uncharitable on several counts. The French are given unjust credit for the French bean (*Phaseolus vulgaris*). Like the runner bean (*P. coccineus*), it is a plant from tropical America and the only real part the French played in its history is that they seem to have been the first Europeans to take to it as a vegetable after it was brought back by the Spanish conquistadors at the end of the sixteenth century. Dwarf bean is

variety 'The Prince'. I was always a bit sceptical; it seemed to me to be more stringy than was good for it so I gradually progressed to the coloured pencil-podded varieties. The yellow so-called wax-pods like 'Mont d'Or' are well worth growing, being versatile, tasty and usable in the kitchen both hot and cold. The purple-podded types aren't; they have little flavour and even lose that rich colour on cooking (in rather the same way that the initially pretty-looking Italian bi-coloured beetroot 'Chioggia' becomes a bland nothing in the pan). My next port of call was with the slender pencil-podded beans often called Kenya beans for no better reason I am sure than that many varieties are grown there commercially (look at the 'country of origin' label when next in your supermarket). I was hooked, first with a variety appropriately called 'Masai' although that has now vanished but others, almost as good, like 'Safari' and 'Opera' have followed. They are high-yielding, long-cropping, tend to hold the pods well clear of the soil and have much the best flavour and crunchy texture of any dwarf beans I have grown. The wait for runner beans is no longer quite so drawn out.

Nonetheless when the wait is over, my supreme loyalty remains. But you must have fun with your runner bean growing. I never stop reminding people that they were first grown in Europe as ornamentals and a mixture of varieties with red, white and bi-coloured flowers adds hugely to the appearance of the plants. I have

perhaps a more meaningful name. My comments are less relevant today because dwarf bean varieties seem to me to have improved beyond measure in recent seasons, both in quantity and quality. They are divided into two principal groups depending on the shape of the pod: pencil-podded or flat-podded. Most experienced vegetable gardeners would at one time have recommended unreservedly the flat-podded

I mix runner bean varieties with differently coloured flowers for added interest. Here, 'White Emergo' is growing with 'Polestar' and bi-coloured 'Painted Lady'.

tended to settle on the red-flowered 'Polestar', the white 'White Emergo' and what was for a long time the only bi-coloured variety 'Painted Lady', although there is now at least one other. 'Sunset', which I haven't yet grown, is pink. As with peas, I use a ridge tent pattern support, although with 3m/10ft canes. I space the canes 30cm/12in apart with an intermediate supporting string mid-way between each. (If canes are placed 15cm/6in apart, the whole structure begins to look like a lion cage; and requires twice as many canes.) I sow two beans at the base of each support (every 15cm/6in therefore) and remove the weaker if both emerge. But yes, I do sow directly. Beans aren't plants that relish root disturbance and so growing them in pots for transplanting doesn't make sense to me. By mid-spring when I sow, the soil is quite warm enough for germination – an argument in favour of transplanting was that bean (and pea) seed will rot if it is allowed to stay for more than about a week in cold soil. But now that springs are generally warmer, that argument falls.

I have never subscribed to the view that low-growing plants are ideal for small gardens. Numerous seed catalogues still suggest just that, however, advocating the short-growing runner bean varieties like 'Hammond's Dwarf Scarlet',

White rot can soon turn a decent onion into something rotten and useless, although red-skinned varieties seem to be less prone.

Pickwick' or 'Hestia'. In practice, in a tiny garden where space is limited, the greatest benefit derives from a plant that grows upwards, not sideways; rather as the confined area of Manhattan gave succour to the skyscraper. And indeed, by that token, if your space is really confined, you might want to try climbing French beans ('climbing dwarf beans' doesn't sound right) such as 'Cobra'.

No cook worthy of the name can manage without onions or their close relatives: shallots, garlic, chives and, to a lesser extent, leeks. Chives aside, which are plants for the herb garden, they all have drawbacks. They are among the slowest growing of vegetables – the first seeds I sow every year (on or around New Year's Day) are onions and so they occupy the ground for a long period. They are also relatively inexpensive to buy and the shop-bought article is of excellent flavour – indistinguishable from home-grown. They are also prone to several diseases of which the most significant is white rot. This is especially serious on the plants that gardeners call spring onions but

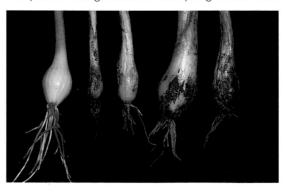

commercial growers called salad onions, and it causes a white fluffy mould at the base of the bulbs, rendering the whole plant completely useless. Even more importantly, it is ineradicable and will persist in the soil almost indefinitely. If you haven't by now been dissuaded from onions, however, choose some red-skinned as well as white-skinned onions for their milder flavour (and generally better resistance to white rot). Sow bulb onions in modules for planting out later and, unless you want showbench-sized bulbs, place four seeds into each module and keep them as a group of four throughout their lives. This is a classic instance of using close spacing to regulate plant size. Instead of one large bulb, you will produce four smaller ones, of much greater use in the kitchen.

Relatively few gardeners grow leeks but those who do generally transplant them and a belief has grown up that this is essential. It isn't. Leeks can be sown direct and provided you are content with moderately sized plants, this makes much sense. By contrast, shallots are traditionally grown from small bulbs called sets and, although there has been a trend in recent years for seed companies to offer shallot seeds, I don't find this way of growing them as successful and can't see the logic behind it. Planting shallots is about as easy a vegetable planting task as you will ever have. You

A plank laid across the bed helps protect the soil when I am planting module-grown clumps of onions.

simply push them into the soil with the wispy bits showing and hope the local blackbirds don't decide to play tug-of-war with them.

I have touched on the use of close sowing to regulate onion size and this is something worthy of greater consideration. Another approach to saving room in the kitchen garden is to ignore most of the conventional wisdom about plant spacing that you will read on seed packets and basic gardening books and to grow the plants much closer together. The spacings that are generally recommended will, by and large, give the you the largest individual plants but they might not give you the largest yield per unit area. This is because, all other things being equal, the size that plants – and especially vegetables – will attain is a function of their spacing, which dictates the degree of competition between them. Visitors commonly remark on how closely I space potatoes particularly; perhaps their nature makes close spacing more obvious. Instead of the 60 x 30cm/24 x 12in and 75 x 30cm/30 x 12in for early

and maincrop respectively, I plant all potatoes a trowel's length apart each way (my trowel is 30cm/12in long). And indeed, equidistant spacing of almost all vegetable crops will invariably give you a greater yield per unit area than jamming them close together in rows with wide open spaces between the rows where weeds will thrive. The row-cropping of vegetables is a largely outdated practice that had its origin in the eighteenth century when vegetable farmers simply mimicked what cereal farmers did. But cereal farmers were only growing their crops in rows because a man named Jethro Tull had invented a horse-drawn seed drill and a horse-drawn hoe that required this method of growing. The hoe cleared the weeds between the rows but the plants had to be sown in rows to make this work. There's absolutely no justification for twenty-first century vegetable gardeners to do the same. Weeding vegetables with a hand hoe working from either side of a plot of equidistantly spaced plants is certainly no hardship.

FRUIT

I have said we are totally self-sufficient in almost all soft fruit; certainly this is true of blackcurrants, red currants, white currants, gooseberries, blackberries and hybrid berries. We grow all our soft fruit in a fruit cage; needs must because we have a large and voracious bird population in the village which would otherwise rapidly reduce my efforts to naught. The fruit cage is 4 x 3m/13 x 10ft and

within it, we have our seven self-sufficient crops. There's no mystery to achieving this. It is simply a matter of training the plants in the most productive manner and of avoiding the most vigorous varieties. I grow one double cordon plant each of the gooseberry varieties 'Invicta' and 'Lord Derby', two of the redcurrant 'Stanza', one of the white currant 'White Versailles', two bushes of the compact blackcurrant 'Ben Sarek' (blackcurrants can't be grown as cordons), a 1.5m/5ft row of 'Autumn Bliss' raspberry and, along the south and west-facing sides, 2m/6½ft of blackberry 'Ashton Cross' and 2m/6½ft of 'Medana Tayberry'.

Summer-fruiting raspberries don't grow well here and so I now grow only the autumn fruiting 'Autumn Bliss' which crops extraordinarily prolifically, with the welcome bonus of fresh raspberries maturing at exactly the time of year when most other people have grown weary of them. I commend 'Autumn Bliss' but do so with the reminder that it is a primocane variety – it bears its fruit on the tips of the canes of the current year and must therefore be pruned at a different time. All canes should be cut to soil level in late winter, unlike the selective pruning out of old fruiting canes that should be done after cropping with summer fruiting varieties. It is also a vigorous plant whose canes will emerge some distance away from the row and even from the fruit cage. Ideally, they should be pulled up while wearing strong gloves but they are also tough and chopping them off with a spade is more practicable, even if it means that they are more likely to sprout again.

I have grown strawberries but presently don't. To grow strawberries successfully, they need to be treated as long-rotation vegetables, and this takes up a great deal of room. Most varieties decline significantly in cropping after the first season and the notion that, as garden plants, they are really perennials is quite fallacious. It surprises many people to realize that the typical modern supermarket strawberry, imported from Spain, has probably been grown as an annual. These varieties are called day-neutral. They originated in California and, unlike the traditional European strawberries, their flowering and fruiting are not dependent on day length but on temperature; in warm climates or in greenhouses, they fruit virtually continuously. But they must be grown as annuals because the second year crop is small indeed and this serves as a useful reminder that all strawberries decline in yield after the first season.

When we moved to our current garden in 1983, we had four apple trees: an ancient and relatively rotten 'Ellison's Orange', (a lovely early dessert apple that has since succumbed to a combination of fungus, a heavy crop and strong winds) and mature, old specimens of the cookers 'Bramley's Seedling', 'Stirling Castle' (an old, early variety that produces wonderful apple sauce) and 'Catshead' (a huge tree of an old Gloucestershire variety with gigantic fruit that are as dangerous as

coconuts if you sit underneath when they are dropping). There was also a 'Victoria' plum that then and now gives the impression of being held together with string and sealing wax. Today, in only a slightly larger space, we have twenty-nine apple varieties, four pears, two plums and an apricot, with some interesting and attractive features to boot. The knack, just as with soft fruit, is to choose an appropriate training system.

Most of the apples are grown in one of two ways. I have a tunnel 8m/26ft long and 1.2m/4ft wide that bisects the kitchen garden. Along it are planted matching pairs of ten different apple varieties trained as espaliers, in order of flowering and fruiting: the earliest, 'Irish Peach', at one end and the latest, 'Pitmaston Pineapple', at the other. The blossom opens in a wave along the tunnel over a period of about two weeks and it is one of

In addition to being an attractive feature of my kitchen garden, the fruit tunnel enables me to grow a wide range of apple varieties in a small area.

the most admired features in the garden. I also have a line of twelve further apples trained as single cordons at one side of the kitchen garden, again in order of fruiting. The pears form yet another boundary to the kitchen garden, separating it from the main lawn. They too are trained as espaliers (probably the best of all pear training systems) and comprise, in order of maturity, 'Beurre Hardy', 'Williams Bon Chrétien',

'Williams Bon Crétien' is the second of of four pear varieties maturing successively in my kitchen garden.

'Doyenné du Comice' and 'Conference'. The additional plum is 'Marjorie's Seedling', trained as a fan against the outside of the fruit cage, the apricot is 'Moorpark', fan-trained against a warm wall and reasonably successful. Apricots are much hardier than most people imagine. I have always suspected that their reputation for tenderness comes because my generation grew up believing they don't occur in gardens, only in tins. It is a replacement for a peach which, like almost all outdoor peaches in this country, was a martyr to peach leaf curl disease. The other principal addition is a little tree of the wonderful crab apple 'John Downie' on the dwarfing rootstock M27 in a large terracotta pot. Although the rootstock restricts its height to 1.3m/4¼ft, it has grown there contentedly in John Innes No. 3 potting compost for sixteen years (although fed regularly of course) and yields more than enough fruit to enable us to stock up annually with crab apple jelly.

HERBS

For any half-decent cook, herbs are essential plants and they seem to epitomize modern man (and woman) in the kitchen. Despite the fact that they are on sale in every garden centre and shop as well as specialist herb nurseries, less experienced gardeners still seem unsure exactly what they are – or which they should grow. Thyme is generally recognized as a kitchen herb, but what about parsley? Sage is generally perceived as a herb but what about onion? And where do lettuce and celery fit in? Where do vegetables end and herbs begin? I don't know, and so I've devised my own definitions and as far as culinary use is concerned, I include only those plants that are used principally to add specific flavours to dishes and meals without being major edible components in their own right. So parsley and some types of onion are in; lettuce and celery are out.

Most garden herbs originate from warm dry climates, the Mediterranean especially. They will generally succeed best therefore in the sunniest part of the garden and on a light well-drained soil.

Among common herbs, only mint is really successful in partial shade. If your garden soil is naturally light or sandy, therefore, herbs will usually thrive without any major attention to the soil although on a clay site, it is essential to incorporate organic matter to lighten it. In practice, as herb gardens need only be fairly small (see below), the simplest answer on a really heavy, difficult site is often to construct a raised bed for them or to use a number of large containers. As with vegetables, the soil for herbs should preferably be around neutral although the pH is not critical and even fairly strongly alkaline or acid conditions will still enable you to produce satisfactory results.

I find an area of about 4m²/43 square feet is adequate for a good representative range of the important types of culinary herb. My own preference is largely to restrict the herb garden itself to the culinary types and to use other herbs within other garden plantings – the mixed border, for instance, where their attractiveness and/or fragrance will be particularly valuable. It is most important nonetheless, to position any dedicated herb garden close to the kitchen – herbs are always best freshly picked and any cook will rightly soon become frustrated at having to walk more than a few strides every time a dish is prepared.

The arrangement of the plants in a herb garden can be informal (simply placing the taller types at the back and the smaller to the front) although many gardeners find a formal style more attractive, mimicking the regimented herb gardens that have been used since medieval times. One popular version of the formal planting is to arrange the plants in a cartwheel pattern, using either a real cartwheel and planting the herbs between the spokes, or constructing a facsimile wheel – from bricks for instance. I don't know who first dreamed up this idea but I wish they hadn't bothered as I think it looks simply dreadful. Whatever scheme is used, do bear in mind the need to reach all parts of the bed easily for picking the plants – stepping stones are useful in a large area.

My short list of essential kitchen herbs with my recommended varieties is:

Chives (*Allium schoenoprasum*)

Small, clump-forming, perennial relative of the onion. Buy a potted plant, put it in the centre of your herb bed and provided it doesn't succumb to rust disease, it will be with you, attractively flowering every spring, for years.

Dill (*Anethum graveolens*)

Annual. Imparts an aniseed flavour but is gentler than fennel. Sow it like chervil and coriander in the kitchen garden but I find it is best sown in a clump rather than in rows as it is then easier to support.

I've often thought that if people were told chives was a rare plant from China, they'd be content to pay handsomely for it as an ornamental.

Chervil (*Anthriscus cerefolium*)

Annual. It resembles cow parsley but is only about 60cm/24in tall. Sow it among the lettuces and radishes of your kitchen garden and enjoy the fragrance as you brush against it.

Horseradish (*Armoracia rusticana*)

Perennial. Highly invasive. Grow it in a confined bed made with old paving slabs or in a large container about 60cm/24in in diameter. Each autumn, dig up as much as you like for grating to produce horseradish sauce. You will unavoidably leave behind plenty of root fragments, which will grow again to produce next season's crop.

Tarragon (*Artemisia dracunculus*)

Perennial. A somewhat fragile looking plant with rather delicate upright shoots and soft, narrowly willow-like leaves. *A. dracunculus* is the true

French tarragon and with protection will grow almost everywhere. There is no justification therefore for using the larger, coarser but hardier Russian tarragon (*A. d. dracunculoides*) which is sometimes offered.

Coriander (*Coriandrum sativum*)

Annual. A bit like chervil although taller and not as hardy. Grow it in a similar way but be aware that it is taller and prone to being knocked over by wind and rain so some loose wrap-around support makes sense.

Fennel (*Foeniculum vulgare*)

Perennial. A tall, feathery plant with pretty little yellow flowers. The bronze form (usually called, rather unimaginatively, 'Bronze Form' but now, more accurately, 'Giant Bronze') has attractive, olive-green foliage but produces both green and bronze seedlings. It is a big plant and you will only need one.

Bay/Sweet bay (*Laurus nobilis*)

Shrub. Bay is the largest important herb plant: a tall evergreen bush or small tree. While you are growing bay, you may as well grow it attractively so buy a relatively inexpensive small plant, put it in an ornamental pot of John Innes No. 3 compost

PAGE 68: You only need a short row of dill to provide leaf and seeds for a season's use. PAGE 69: One plant of the herb fennel is sufficient, so why not choose the bronze-foliaged form?

and train it as a standard. After a few years you will have the satisfaction of knowing you have produced something that would cost serious money at a garden centre.

Mint (*Mentha* spp.)

Perennials. They are particularly invasive so grow in them sunken pots of John Innes No. 2 compost. *M.* x *gracilis* (ginger mint); *M.* x *piperita* (black peppermint); *M. spicata* (spearmint – the best for new potatoes); *M. spicata* var. *crispa* (curly mint); *M. suaveolens* (and its variegated form 'Variegata') (apple mints – the best for mint sauce); *M.* x *villosa* 'Alopecuroides' (Bowles' mint – also good for mint sauce).

Basil (*Ocimum basilicum*)

Annual. There are now ten or twelve excellent forms available from seed. Sow them in 20cm-/10in-diameter terracotta pots of John Innes No.1 compost and be especially careful to keep them on the dry side: they are highly prone to damping off soon after germination. As well as the normal broad-leaved, try the purple-leaved varieties derived from *O. basilicum* var. *purpurascens*, the lemon-scented varieties of *Ocimum* x *citriodorum* and the compact *Ocimum minimum* (bush or Greek basil).

Marjoram/oregano (Origanum spp.)

Perennial. Low growing, clump forming, slightly woody perennials with 60–80cm/24–30in leafy stems arising annually from the base. European varieties of *O. vulgare* (oregano) are more strongly flavoured than the wild British form. The golden leaved form 'Aureum' (gold marjoram) is especially attractive. *O. majorana* (sweet marjoram) and *O. onites* (pot marjoram) are similar and occur in a range of varieties including an attractive crinkle-leaved type of *O. onites*.

Parsley (*Petroselinum crispum*)

Biennial. Sow seed in spring and again in late summer. The curled types are given names such as 'Moss Curled' or 'Curlina'; the alternatives are 'Plain Leaved' forms (*P. c.* var. *neapolitanum*), which are taller plants (60cm/24in) with flat, dark-green leaves and a stronger flavour.

Rosemary (*Rosmarinus officinalis*)

Shrub. An evergreen that can be clipped to attractive shapes and even low hedges. Several varieties exist with pink and white flowers as well as a range in the intensity of the blue. Ornamental forms also occur in a range of habits from more or less prostrate ('Prostratus' or 'Severn Sea') to upright ('Miss Jessup's Upright') but for culinary use, the normal species is satisfactory.

Sage (*Salvia officinalis*)

Perennial. A rather lax woody plant. There are several attractive foliage variants, all equally good in the kitchen, including 'Purpurascens' with purple leaves, 'Purpurascens Variegata' with variegated purple leaves and 'Icterina', a golden variegated form.

Thyme (*Thymus* spp.)

Perennial. Small woody perennials in a wide range of types with a range of leaf variegations, habit and flowers. The small bush form *T. vulgaris* 'Silver Posie' is much the best culinary thyme.

One of the popular myths about herb growing is that towards the end of the second or third year, you should start to divide or take cuttings as the plants become woody and 'tired'. Unless you have immeasurably more time than I have, I suggest you do no such thing. By all means accept that herbs aren't long-term perennials, but save yourself the trouble, spend a few pounds and buy some new plants in the spring that have been propagated from good vigorous stock not from some clapped-out individuals you have been cutting and pulling for two or more years.

Another common question I am asked is. Aren't the pots of herbs you can buy in supermarkets and which might last a few weeks on your window sill just as good? No, they are all grown from seed (which excludes many of the best varieties of most herbs) and they have been forced in greenhouses. They are soft, generally pretty tasteless and for the most dire emergency use only.

GARDENING WITH
ORNAMENTALS

GARDENING WITH ORNAMENTALS

I doubt if anyone gardens solely to produce food. A man in the village close to where I live has a garden which I drive past regularly. It is entirely given over to leeks. But even he has a few containers of annuals at strategic intervals. So, to a greater or, in his case, a seriously lesser degree, ornamental gardening is of interest to all of us. But attractive planting can be achieved in a wide variety of ways; and let's never forget that attractiveness is all in the eye of the beholder. For all I know, it may even be that those few hundred leeks are there principally for the rich glaucous colour of their foliage. I don't want to dictate but having sampled almost every way of bringing attraction to my own garden over the years, and for my own reasons rejected many, I hope my experiences will be of value.

I have already looked at the rather special category of trees and shrubs in Chapter Two and so here I want to consider the uses and relative merits of non-woody ornamentals – annuals and herbaceous perennials, and their special subdivisions into bulbs and alpines.

ANNUALS

Like most gardeners, I have vacillated over the years in my attitude to annuals. As children we loved growing them from seed because results came quickly and rewardingly. In our early gardening lives, most of us then went through phases of considering them rather vulgar, unsubtle and redolent of public park plantings; and we devoted ourselves to the maxims of the Hardy Plant Society instead. But if I

am typical of gardeners at large, we then returned and realized that they have their own, special part to play in gardens and that among them are plants that offer a form, habit, colour or simple abundance of flowers that few perennials could approach. And in the case of the winter-flowering pansy, they offer us something totally without peer in providing brightness and colour in the cold, dark months. Every annual I grow today is in a container of some sort. But I think this situation has arisen more because of my fondness for containers than any specific view about growing annuals. It is true that, in a bed or border, they require more work, leaving a big untidy gap when they are removed at the end of the season, especially if any perennials around them have adjusted their own growth and shape accordingly. Three examples from my garden today will indicate how and why I think at least some annuals make sense in any garden. Firstly, one of the more improbable of all my plantings.

The African marigold, despite its name, is derived from a Mexican plant called *Tagetes erecta*; the French marigold from another Mexican plant called *T. patula*. It always used to be said that the African varieties were tall and the French dwarf, while medium-sized hybrids between them were known as Afro-French marigolds. I think

---

RIGHT: Eschscholzias provide a stunning splash of colour – and are surprisingly durable perennials.
PAGES 76–7: Universal pansies are without peer if it is colourful flowers in the winter that you seek.

much of the real ancestry and nomenclature has been forgotten however because there are now F1 hybrid dwarf African marigolds only 30cm/12in tall. They absolutely personify hot, vibrant oranges and yellows; they are not subtle plants. But every year, I have a terracotta pot filled with one of the most vividly orange dwarf doubles and place it close to the most formal and traditional area of my garden – the box, yew and gravel of my knot garden. That splash of orange close to those rich dark greens creates a stunning effect no perennial could mimic. And the combination isn't even as historically daft as it might seem because my knot garden is based loosely on a design from the early 1500s, the same century in which the ancestral *Tagetes* species first arrived in Britain.

A second example: I have a small 'walk-through' gravel garden where I grow plants of Mediterranean type – grasses, dry climate sedges, some dwarf lavenders, inevitably a few terracotta containers of scented and ornamental-leaved pelargoniums, which I adore and which are everywhere in my garden in summer, and that now well-known but still stunning and remarkable tall and wiry purple-flowered South American plant *Verbena bonariensis* that, amazingly, was first introduced to Britain as long ago as 1737. It's the type of planting made familiar on a much larger scale through the enterprise of Beth Chatto at her garden in Essex. At either end, I wanted larger containers containing something appropriate to make a statement. I had, however, grown rather

weary of yuccas and other spiky so-called architectural plants such as you will see for instance in the Mediterranean area at Hidcote in Gloucestershire (one of the few flaws, I always think, in that otherwise wonderful and hugely important garden). Also, I wanted plants that would be appropriate towards the end of summer and into the autumn, as the grass and sedge flowers were turning from green to gold. I finally found my answer in 2002 with an annual. *Rudbeckia* 'Cherokee Sunset' isn't a plant for which I would automatically make a bee-line in the seed catalogues, if for no other reason than that it has won gold medals and other awards in various seed

LEFT: I make no apologies for associating the formal greens of my knot garden with an assertive pot of orange marigolds. ABOVE: Rudbeckia 'Cherokee Sunset' has been one of my annual plant discoveries of recent seasons.

trials. These accolades generally seem go to something I can't stand, such as a picotee petunia or a rainbow-coloured pansy. But this British-bred *Rudbeckia* is altogether different; about 60cm/24in tall it has a blend of double and semi-double flowers in quite wonderful autumnal bronzes and golds. Massed in a big tub, it is stunning and is, I am told, likely to be followed by other new varieties of similar type. To use a hackneyed phrase in plant breeding: a real breakthrough.

Finally, let me describe another annual planting inspired by someone else's garden, not this time a great garden or one planted by a great designer, but one that is simply famous for being famous. Claude Monet's garden at Giverny in Normandy is among the most photographed and familiar anywhere, almost entirely because of its water lily ponds that provided the inspiration for some of the best-known paintings in the world. They are pretty enough in their way and interesting for their historical association. But retrace your steps back through the tunnel under the road towards Monet's house and you will find something much more striking and relevant. Athwart a broad, roped-off gravel path is a wide metal arch bedecked with roses, a structure that has become known as a Giverny arch. As summer advances, the gravel is gradually submerged in a carpet of nasturtiums that creep inwards from the soil beds at the side. By late summer the effect is stunning. I don't have a gravel bed as wide and I don't have a Giverny arch but I do have beds close to the house where nasturtiums, in all the astonishing variety now available, similarly spread and tumble over a low wall to produce a truly wonderful effect that can be viewed from the kitchen windows. I am both surprised and delighted that the incredible array of yellows, creams, whites, browns, oranges and reds in single, semi-double and double forms, all seem to come true from seed and the whole area requires no re-sowing as everything self-seeds each season with wonderful abandon. They also make delightful cut flowers for a small vase on the kitchen table, lasting only two or three days but then easily renewed. In passing, I must add that I am always slightly puzzled at the frequency with which the nasturtium (*Tropaeolum majus* mostly, although with other species thrown in) is listed in seed catalogues as a hardy annual. It certainly doesn't look hardy when the first frosts of winter flatten it in my garden.

PERENNIALS

Perennials have many virtues and they certainly have a much longer life-span than the one season of annuals but I sometimes have to remind gardeners that being perennial isn't the same as being immortal. Perennials don't last forever, and they certainly won't last for long in any sort of productive condition without care and attention. In everyday gardening language, 'perennial' has come to be synonymous with 'herbaceous perennial' and with something that dies down in the autumn. This is a pity because it obscures the

close relationship and similarity between the deciduous herbaceous perennial and the evergreen herbaceous perennial; between the deciduous herbaceous perennial and those forms of it that happen to have underground storage organs and are generally called bulbs, and between all of these and the diverse group of plants called alpines.

Herbaceous Perennials

The herbaceous perennial is, I think, simultaneously one of the most useful and one of the most troublesome of plants in the modern garden. I feel duty bound to put them some way behind shrubs (although well ahead of annuals) in their requirements for continuing attention. Like

I have very few all-perennial borders. There just aren't enough hours in the season to maintain them properly.

annuals, herbaceous perennials ostensibly provide you with nothing in the winter. In reality, many offer much appeal, certainly until the New Year, because their dead fruiting heads (seed heads) can be at least as attractive as their flowers and, bedecked with cobwebs and dew or rime, can be almost magical. Generally, by early January, however, a combination of birds and winter weather means they are becoming unsightly and should then be cut back.

Herbaceous perennials must be used with care in the garden because on the whole they are relatively large plants. (There are a great many small herbaceous perennials but they are usually called, and sold as, alpines, irrespective of whether they originated anywhere near a mountain.) The large size means that the gap they leave out of season is also a large one. In times past, but rarely today, whole and vast borders were devoted solely to such plants. The so-called herbaceous border, much loved of Gertrude Jekyll and her nineteenth- and early-twentieth-century contemporaries was, at its best, in summer, one of the greatest glories the English garden has ever seen. But such a feature slowly, understandably and quite rightly fell from favour, partly through its enormous labour intensiveness and partly through its depressing appearance in winter. While a huge, dead area of soil might be overlooked in the extensive grounds of a country house, it would occupy an unacceptably large slice of the plot of the modern home gardener.

Today, therefore, herbaceous perennials are seldom planted in beds or borders to the exclusion of other plants. Most commonly, they are integrated with shrubs in what has become known as the mixed border, the shrubs providing a permanent above-ground framework. But gardeners nonetheless go wrong because they forget some basic rules of planting. It is still important to select varieties with complementary colours and flowering times, to choose carefully the taller varieties for planting at the back and sides of the border – with the lower-growing ones in the centre and front – and to choose perennials that will complement in all respects the appearance of the shrubs. But, above all, don't expect to get it right first time. I never have and I defy anyone else to produce a planting that includes herbaceous perennials and that doesn't require some to be moved at the end of the first season because their growth rate was underestimated or their colour wasn't exactly what was expected.

Quite possibly this will be due to the labels being little help. As mentioned previously, I have something of a bee in my bonnet about plant labels. Some are undeniably helpful and accurate; most aren't. Admittedly, hardy plant labels tend to be better than those accompanying house plants where the ultimate in useless advice was provided by one that

Perennials are superficially attractive for a few weeks, but labour intensive. The adjective 'perennial' is more applicable to the work than the appeal.

suggested 'Please put me somewhere nice'. I think it lost a little in translation from the Dutch.

Seed catalogues have large sections devoted to herbaceous perennials and it may be thought therefore that raising them from seed is the best way to produce them. In general, I find that it is not. Largely I say this because the best varieties – in the sense of most attractive or functionally

It is a sad fact that some of my favourite herbaceous plants – like these verbascums – are some of the shortest-lived.

useful – can't usually be raised in this manner. They must be propagated vegetatively and thus must be purchased from nurseries or garden centres as plants. I must add one rather important group of exceptions, however. For many people (myself included), there is an appeal in growing plants in their wild form and there are many species that have never been subjected to hybridization and selection and exist only in their natural, unaltered state. A great many, indeed the majority among them, do not have the widespread appeal that attracts them to those nurserymen who cater for the mass market. Inevitably, therefore, plants of these species should either be sought from specialist suppliers or you should raise them yourself from seed (which may themselves have to be obtained from a specialist rather than a mass-market company). By and large, you will succeed best if you sow them in the same way as hardy annuals but always grow on the young plants in pots for at least a season before planting them out in the garden. This will ensure they are robust and have a strong enough root and crown system to enable them to survive.

I want to make a few points about evergreen herbaceous perennials. The concept of the evergreen habit usually tends to be applied to trees and shrubs – most deciduous types lose their leaves at the end of the summer wherever they happen to be growing and most evergreens don't. Because an evergreen woody plant retains its leaves it appears more or less the same all year round. By contrast, most so-called evergreen perennials, which tend to be monocotyledonous (*Kniphofia*, or red hot poker, is a familiar example), can often become browned and appear frayed and untidy in winter. This can be avoided by giving them additional protection, but this is something to which I have never subscribed. Either a plant is hardy enough to be grown outdoors in your garden or it isn't, and having plants embalmed for the winter in bubble-wrap plastic sheet, or even natural materials such as straw or hessian seems to me pointless. An illustrative recent example is the most common of the Australasian tree ferns, *Dicksonia antarctica*, which has become popular as a garden plant and is sold at garden centres as dormant trunks, priced by the foot. In its native habitat, it is evergreen. In many parts of Britain, however, its fronds turn brown in winter and are generally then cut off and packed around the top of the trunk, tied down and held in place with some form of sheet. They look both ridiculous and unsightly. I defer to no one in my fondness for tree ferns but I also defer to no one in wanting my garden to be attractive in winter and I am not interested in gift-wrapped vegetation. My tree ferns, therefore, are in the greenhouse and if I didn't have room for them there, I wouldn't have any. Nor would I have any other evergreen herbaceous perennial that needed any more protection than a mound of compost over the crown. This brings me rather conveniently to grasses, many of which are evergreen, fully hardy and most attractive.

Grasses

Considered in respect of the way they grow and their appearance when growing, grasses fall into two main groups. On the one hand there are the spreading or tillering grasses (a tiller is a shoot that grows from a stem base). Collectively they merge together to form a mat and if the mat is big enough we call it a lawn. On the other hand there are the clump-forming species which grow more or less as discrete individuals – envisage the habit of pampas grass and you will have the correct image. By definition, even modestly vigorous spreading grasses will sooner or later become a problem in a border; or indeed almost anywhere other than a lawn. I am constantly surprised at how widely available and popular is the highly aggressive striped grass *Phalaris arundinacea* var. *picta*, commonly known as gardener's garters. I have even known couch grass take it on and come away somewhat chastened. Clump-forming grasses are quite another matter, however, and, allowing for the inclusion of the superficially similar sedges and rushes, many hundreds of species and varieties, annual and perennial are now available.

Almost none require winter protection and for many, the appeal of their persisting seed heads in autumn and winter is at least as great as that in summer. They are indispensable inhabitants of the gravel garden (see page 79) but have many other applications in borders, as individual specimens (and a specimen grass needn't always mean pampas grass) and even in containers. I add a few more to my collection every year and am seldom disappointed – although the disappointment, if it does come, is usually with some of the paler golden variegated varieties, which tend to be rather less hardy, rather more prone to decline in heavier soils and somewhat more susceptible to losing their initially promising colours.

Among the enormous number of ornamental grasses and sedges with golden, variegated or other coloured leaves and with modest growth ambitions and decent behaviour that I particularly enjoy are:

Carex brunnea 'Variegata'
A small tufted sedge with golden leaf margins, sometimes grown as a house plant and said to be a bit tender but it is hardy enough in my garden provided the soil is well-drained.

Carex oshimensis 'Evergold'
One of the most familiar of all golden species with a yellow-cream central leaf stripe.

Deschampsia flexuosa 'Tatra Gold'
Very narrow, spiky leaves, bright yellow when they first emerge but later softening in colour.

One of my stone troughs is home to a small collection of sempervivums – and of necessity contains almost no soil.

Festuca glauca 'Golden Toupee'
One of many forms of the best of all blue grasses, although this variety is suffused with gold. The leaves are tightly rolled and almost rush-like.

Pennisetum alopecuroides 'Hameln'
Graceful foliage with pretty but extremely spiky flower heads in late summer.

Uncinia rubra
Slightly larger than most of my other recommendations and with rich dark red foliage.

Alpines
I was once asked to define an alpine plant and, only slightly facetiously, suggested it was a perennial smaller than its label. The fact is that many alpines have long names and correspondingly big labels, and in modern gardening they seem to me to have little else in common except their smallness. It's always been true that they are a large and diverse group of plants in a large number of different

families. Traditionally, they also had in common an origin in some mountainous region, though certainly not necessarily the Alps. Much of this seems to have gone by the board and many alpine nurseries now simply offer a range of small perennials so if it is real mountain plants that you want, check the identity and do a little homework first.

Perhaps the commonest misconception about alpine plants is that their most important requirement is cold conditions – after all, mountain tops have snow on them. The reality is that alpine plants are tolerant of cold conditions but it is their relative intolerance of high humidity that is much more significant. Yes, of course, it both rains and snows in the mountains and overall precipitation is high. But a drying wind blows too and the soil is thin and free-draining. The enemy of alpine plants is not warmth but clinging damp. Even a hot English June day will do them no harm; in the thin air and cloudless skies of an alpine summer, the sun's heat reflected from exposed rock surfaces can give rise to extremely high temperatures, far in excess of anything they might encounter at sea level.

Where will you grow your alpines? If they are true alpines, not in your mixed border; not even at the front. You must adhere to that requirement for free drainage and this is most easily satisfied, yet again, by a container. Because an alpine collection will probably comprise a considerable number of small plants, none needing deep soil, the relatively shallow stone or replica stone trough has become a *sine qua non* for alpine growing. The growing medium is usually satisfied by a mixture of equal parts of John Innes No. 2 or 3 potting compost and sharp grit but I stress again the importance of checking the requirement of your plants. Some will require strongly acidic and some strongly alkaline conditions so the mixture should be modified as appropriate. Some also require even greater drainage and the growing medium I use for sempervivums and their kind is one of ninety per cent sharp grit with ten per cent John Innes No. 2 potting compost and a topping of crushed slate.

If you want more than a handful of alpine plants, the answer isn't a bigger trough or, as is often found, a rock garden. The eccentric Yorkshireman Reginald Farrer, who all but invented modern alpine gardening, was scathing in his condemnation of so-called rock gardens, most of which he thought looked frankly ridiculous. I largely concur with his view, and unless you have a real rock outcrop or sufficient time, money and inventiveness to create something that looks like one, your alpines are much better grown in an alpine house. Unlike most types of greenhouse, this can be inexpensive to buy and costs almost nothing to run as it requires no artificial heat. It simply needs strong staging to support the gravel beds in which the pots of plants are sunk, a door at each end and more than the usual number of ventilators to provide thorough air movement.

Many alpine plants are fairly easy to grow; many of those that originate from places with specific and unusual soil or climatic features are not, but I am surprised how often gardeners fail even with common and straightforward types because they have overlooked (or have not been told) one simple fact. When you buy an alpine plant, it will be in a small plant pot of soil-less compost (formally peat-based but now more likely of a peat substitute). Treating it simply as any other small perennial, most of us plant it into our alpine bed or trough with the ball of compost relatively intact. And in due course the plant rots away and dies and our enthusiasm for alpine gardening takes a severe knock. It's perfectly understandable that the nursery should have germinated the seed or struck the cutting in compost and grown on the plant in it because that is usually the best way to start things. But once the plant has started to grow, that ball of compost in the garden will soon act as a sump and attract and retain moisture around the roots with inevitable consequences. The drier and freer draining the plant's natural habitat, the quicker will it fail. Perhaps the extreme examples are the species and varieties of *Sempervivum* and *Jovibarba* which grow naturally in the smallest of rock crevices, or, in the case of some of the most familiar forms, commonly called house leeks, on the roofs of buildings. They are undeniably attractive and are bought in a flush of admiration and enthusiasm only to fail in their first season. The answer is so simple. Before you plant your new alpine acquisition, remove it from the pot and wash the compost from its roots.

I learned by accident that leucojums are as responsive as snowdrops to being transplanted in leaf.

Bulbs

If you believe some promotional literature and catalogues, bulbs are the answer to every gardener's prayer. They offer flowers of superb quality within a few months of being planted and they do so with the absolute minimum of care and attention. What many gardeners don't realize however is that, while notionally perennial, bulbs can all but exhaust their food reserves after one season's efforts and to have anything like a repeat performance in subsequent years needs a considerable amount of attention on our part. And in some instances it is in any event, I think, doomed to failure and the plants are best considered as annuals.

The plants that fall into this group have little botanical connection with each other and the appearance of their flowers and above ground growth generally reflects this. What they do have in common lies out of sight below soil level: a swollen and modified part of the root or stem that serves as a food store when the top growth has died down (usually, although not invariably, during the winter). Most are monocotyledons and have the narrow, strap-like leaves characteristic of this group but for gardening purposes it is simplest to think of them all as herbaceous perennials of a rather special type. The difference between a bulb, a corm, a rhizome and a tuber is more of botanical than horticultural interest and indeed some structures once known by one name have recently been reclassified under another. The underground bodies formed by

cyclamen, for instance, were formerly called corms; botanists now call them tubers instead although we still grow them in precisely the same way. In common with general practice, I shall refer to all of these plants as bulbous.

Almost all bulbous plants share one feature. Their swollen underground storage organ is liable to be damaged by pests and is also prone to attack by decay fungi in moist conditions, especially while it is dormant. So although many species can tolerate wet soil when they are in leaf or bloom, they will rapidly succumb if these conditions persist all year round. A heavy clay soil is seldom ideal for them therefore although some localized improvement can be made when planting by laying sand in the base of the planting hole. Growing bulbs in established areas of grass is a popular pastime but should be done with some circumspection. Relatively few types can compete sufficiently well with the grass to thrive; even with daffodils and narcissi, some varieties grow vigorously among grass while others soon fade away. But even those bulbs suitable for

growing in this way should never be planted in lawns or other grass that is constantly mown. A sound general maxim is that the foliage of bulbous plants should be left undisturbed for six weeks after the last flowers fade before cutting it down, something that clearly is quite impossible in mown turf.

The majority of bulbous plants thrive best in full sun and relatively few are tolerant of deep shade; among the significant exceptions suitable for these conditions are those woodland plants like bluebells that produce leaves and flowers early in the year before the tree canopy comes into leaf. Bluebells incidentally are also among the few bulbous plants that can become invasive and must therefore be positioned with caution. I would

ABOVE LEFT: The simplicity of species and near-species tulips has always appealed to me. This is Tulipa orphanidea *Whittallii Group in my gravel garden.*
ABOVE RIGHT: Early-flowering woodland bulbs such as bluebells are dependent on the late-emergence of the tree canopy to obtain the required light to grow.

never plant them in a garden bed or border; they are plants for wilder places. (The wildlife garden bluebell should be the native *Hyacinthoides non-scripta* not the Spanish bluebell (*Hyacinthoides hispanica*), which is the species normally sold for gardens.) In passing, I should add that the other two invasive common bulbs to plant with extreme care are the *Muscari* once called *M. atlanticum* but now *M. neglectum* and the so-called Star-of-Bethlehem *Ornithogalum umbellatum*.

In general, bulbous plants are probably fed less than almost any other type of garden ornamental; and this is one of the main reasons why gardeners so often complain that their plants have failed to bloom after the first year. In that first season, of course, the food reserves in the bulb itself are sufficient to produce a good display of blooms. But to give of their best, bulbs require fertilizer when they are planted in order to help them establish a strong and supportive root system, and most then require feeding annually (preferably with a quick-acting liquid fertilizer) during the six week period after flowering. Only in this way do they stand a chance of building up again the food reserves that enable repeat flowering to take place. Exceptions to this rule are the relatively few varieties of daffodil, crocus, snowdrop and other common bulbs that naturalize readily.

Most reputable bulb suppliers now give full planting directions but there is still considerable confusion in gardeners' minds regarding planting depth. Planting too shallowly is probably the second commonest reason for bulbs to disappoint. A good general rule is to place the bulb with its base at a depth in the soil equal to three times its diameter. Cylindrical hand tools called bulb planters are available at garden centres and work on the principle of removing a plug of soil or turf to produce a hole into which the bulb or bulbs can be placed. In practice, however, I have never found these easy to use, not least because it is difficult to loosen the soil in the base of what is a narrow hole. A trowel or spade, depending on the area involved, is much easier. Although some types of bulb are readily raised from seed using the hardy annual technique, or occasionally by other means, most plants will be bought as dormant bulbs or other storage bodies. After a few years, most will then produce small or daughter bulbs, which take anything from two to about seven years to attain flowering size.

Increasingly, however, I have become aware of the value of planting bulbs in full leaf. For some years, snowdrops have been sold extensively in this way, lifted by the nursery after the flowers have faded. They are usually said to be 'in the green' and are widely recognized as establishing and flowering quicker and more reliably than when planted as dormant bulbs in the autumn. It occurred to me that this has a more general relevance following two events in my own garden, both unintentional. The first occurred when someone well-meaning but relatively inexperienced was assisting me one spring. They thought they were lifting and dividing snowdrops in full leaf after the flowers had faded.

Having seen the results I had to point out to them that they had in fact lifted and divided some snowflakes (*Leucojum*) before they had flowered. But the plants were none the worse for the experience and flowered even better the following year. The second 'happening' involved crown imperials (*Fritillaria imperialis*). Any experienced gardener will tell you they establish slowly, that after planting the bulbs, they can take several seasons to flower fully and that, once they are established, they should be left undisturbed. Some years ago, I had no choice but to lift some one autumn because I was redeveloping a border. I realized I would probably lose two or three years' flowering but there was nothing I could do about it. The bulbs were placed in the bulb store pending re-planting and overlooked. I think it was January when I found them, by which time they had already produced serious shoots. So one mild day I cautiously replanted them, taking care not to damage the new growths; and they flowered that first season as well as they ever had done. Ever since, when buying *Fritillaria* bulbs, I have kept them in store until the shoots appear; I suspect the technique may work with other 'problem' bulbs too.

LEFT: Crown imperials are said to resent disturbance. Wait until the shoots emerge from the bulbs before planting them to encourage early flowering. RIGHT: I always grow large-flowered hybrid tulips for one or at most two years only in containers. This is Tulipa *'Queen of Night'.*

CONTAINER GARDENING

The aspect of my gardening that has gained most in importance over the past twenty-five years is without question my increasing realization of the value of growing plants in containers. Traditionally, as older gardening books will tell you, container planting was essentially of interest and value for people with small courtyard gardens, enabling plants to be grown in places where there is no soil. This is still true, and even larger gardens such as mine have significant areas of what is today called 'hard landscape' – paths, paved areas, terraces

and so forth, on which containers can be placed. But the real revelation hasn't been the increase in planting area container gardening confers, but the increased growing season it affords. And although I use containers extensively in the kitchen garden, it is for ornamental planting that it really scores, with perennials of all kinds as well as with annuals. As I have said countless times, any plant can be grown in a container. It is simply a matter of choosing the right container for each.

Although container gardening is centuries old, it is nonetheless a strange way of going about things. No plants grow naturally in containers (although some do survive in distinctly confined spaces – giving inspiration to the cultivation of bonsai) and I can only assume our ancestors originally did it purely out of curiosity because, unlike the practice of confining animals in stalls and byres, it could never be performed on a large enough scale to replace the growing of plants in the open ground. But having invented it, ancient man would soon have discovered that container growing has both advantages and disadvantages, many of the latter being beyond his wit or resources to counter.

First, the advantages. Containers can be positioned more or less where you wish, free from the need to find an appropriate area of open soil.

Fuschia 'Thalia' is a plant that is best in dappled shade, a requirement most readily satisfied by growing it in a container.

Places in the garden that otherwise would be dull and unproductive can be brightened and used to good purpose. Most importantly, if you have no open garden soil or even no garden, you can benefit from the pleasure and satisfaction that growing plants brings. Containers can be put in conditions that are optimal for the growing of your chosen plants; those that suffer from exposure can be tucked out of the wind; those that suffer from direct sun can be put in dappled shade. Unless they are large and heavy, they can be moved. This offers several benefits. They can be

taken to the greenhouse, potting shed or wherever else is convenient for planting up, free from the limiting factors of the weather. They can even be put at a convenient working level on a potting bench. Mobility means that a container may be placed in its display position when the plants are likely to be at their most attractive and can be moved away again (or even disposed of entirely) once that time is over. All that is really needed is some advance planning, so you have something planted appropriately for different months of the year, and somewhere to store the things as they are moved out of sight.

Gardening in containers also affords you the possibility of growing plants that are wholly unsuited to the type of soil that occurs naturally in your garden. By selecting an appropriate compost, you can grow acid-loving plants in an alkaline district or plants that need a free-draining sandy loam even if your garden soil is better suited to making plates. By and large, the miniature environment in your container will be free from weeds and at least from the majority of the soil-inhabiting pests and diseases that occur in an open garden although I should add that one or two problems, like vine weevil, have made the container environment much their own.

There are, of course, some disadvantages. First, you must use a specially formulated compost because almost all types of garden soil simply don't behave in a container. They lose their structure and become no better than thick

pudding. And whichever type of container and compost you choose, the nutrient content will be finite. Even in the real soil of a real garden, where plants' roots continuously explore new areas, supplementary feeding will be needed sooner or later. In a container, that situation comes even sooner and while soil-less composts may be fine for one season, you really do need a soil-based John Innes potting compost for anything longer. Remember, the higher the John Innes compost number, the longer it will suffice – No. 1 for short-term, No. 2 for medium-term and No. 3 for long-term plantings. But perhaps the biggest of all constraints on container gardening is that of watering. Unable to tap into any moisture reserves, neglected plants in a container will die of water shortage quickly and of course, a hanging basket, with its almost unrestricted drainage, creates the most ridiculous situation of all. Moisture retaining gels in the compost can make a token difference but it is only over the past five years or so that I have finally realized that without an automatic watering system, hanging baskets simply represent gardening for masochists. Not that there is anything complex or costly about automatic watering: an outside tap, a basic watering timer and associated pipe work are not expensive and are simplicity itself to install. If you have other containers fairly close to the hanging basket, it is easy to extend the system with fine-bore hose to provide watering for them all. But it also makes a great deal of common sense to choose plants, especially for smaller containers, that have inherently greater tolerance of dry conditions. A sound maxim to follow is to select those that originate in areas with a Mediterranean climate, like the Mediterranean region itself or South Africa.

SHADE GARDENING

Finally in this chapter I want to give some thought to a topic I've touched on several times already. I confess that until I realized just how many questions I was being asked were concerned with shade, I'd never really thought of it as any more or less significant a factor than the many other environmental variables. But the reality seems to be different. There is a widespread perception that shade is a problem and I'm inclined to think this is simply because less common sense is applied to the matter than to most other aspects of gardening.

You only need walk through a wood to realize shade isn't a huge problem for plant life because,

while there may be fewer plants than in the full sun, and they may be of rather different types, they are certainly there and growing well. It will also be obvious that intensity of shade varies considerably and if you walk from the edge of a wood, where the shade is light (and often dappled), beneath the first trees, where it will be moderate, and finally to the centre of the wood, where it will be deep, you will see a gradual change in the plant species. But instead of thinking about how shaded any given spot is at any given moment, think in terms of the differing total amount of light it receives in the course of twenty-four hours. You will then realize those same variations from light to deep shade in a wood can arise by having an area of a garden shaded for only part of the day – shade for half the morning would constitute light shade, shade for half the day moderate shade and shade for almost the whole day, deep shade. And again by analogy with the wood, you will appreciate that different types of plants will be appropriate for the different situations.

In a garden, the deepest shade is usually to be expected beneath evergreen trees, especially densely foliaged conifers (trying to grow plants beneath yew can be like gardening at night), although while they are in leaf some deciduous species, such as beech, can be almost equally shade casting. Walls will usually produce a deeper

There is nothing difficult about growing plants in shade. It is simply a matter of choosing the most appropriate species.

shade than hedges or fences (which often allow at least some light to pass through, making for a dappled effect) and common sense suggests that the higher the wall, the greater the duration of the shade. A bed adjoining the wall on the darkest side of a house may receive almost no direct sunlight at all.

Light is generally associated with heat, and just as a sunny position is a warm one, so a shaded position will be cooler. But the shadiest position need not necessarily be the place for the most hardy of your plants. Although a fully-shaded aspect will generally be overall the coldest part of

your garden and will receive the least sun, in winter, this may be no bad thing, for the damage caused to plants by winter cold results rather more from the rapidity with which their frozen tissues thaw than from the absolute minimum temperature. So, in reality, plants growing in a less shaded aspect but where they will be at risk of being struck by the early morning sunshine and so thawing out quickly, are likely to suffer more damage than those in a darker one.

Provided the thaw takes place slowly, even seriously frozen tissues needn't be damaged.

**WATER
GARDENING**

WATER GARDENING

Water gardening is horticulture's new rock and roll. But it can be frustratingly difficult to get right and most people who create water gardens try to include too much. Who is to blame for this? Just possibly the manufacturers of water gardening equipment who now produce a bewildering range of pre-formed ponds, pond liners, fountains, waterfalls, underwater lighting, wall features, pebble fountains and much else besides. Or perhaps the great water designers of the past: Grillet, who gave us the Chatsworth cascade, Le Nôtre, who used water to truly remarkable effect at Versailles or the gardening hydrologists who produced such Italian astonishments as the Villa d'Este, Villa Lante or my own favourite, the Palazzo Farnese. I'm the last to deny that water in a garden is not only indispensable but can look fantastic. But never forget that while large-scale gardens do call for large scale water, the more modest modern garden doesn't. That said, the opportunities for using water to enhance the garden have never been greater.

DESIGNING WITH WATER

I have had at least one water feature in all my gardens, my garden today has six and my experience tells me that the gardener who has once had a water feature is unlikely ever to be without one again. The value of water in the garden is easy to define. Visually, it has a special quality that catches the light and catches the eye. Audibly, it is uplifting, the merest, gentlest sound of water movement being sufficient to bring life to any garden landscape.

It can be tantalizing and tempting too. In my own garden and generally in gardens I design for other people, I believe in including an element of surprise, of something a little unexpected to entrance and delight as you turn a corner. Because I also believe almost all water features should involve some movement of the water itself, that element of surprise is harder to cater for; so it is replaced by an element of intrigue. You will hear the water from some distance away but will be tantalized until you can discover its source. I remember many years ago making my first visit to Burford House in Worcestershire, most famously the home of one of the National Collections of Clematis, when its then owner and creator, the late John Treasure guided my tour. Despite the clematis and many other fine plantings, the enduring memory is not of plants but of a deceptive garden, and of water. Many garden designers strive to create the illusion of more space than is really present but few achieve it in the way John Treasure did. You can hear the nearby stream and the River Teme and are aware of the presence of pools but the structure of the garden urges you to go on and on, without ever letting you know whether you are walking in straight lines or circles; and fooling you into not knowing exactly where all that water is. It is truly a most clever garden and one that has inspired my own use of water ever since.

It's a simplistic and apparently pointless truism to say that water has unique properties but, as a structural garden feature, this fact is inescapable.

More than anything else you will put in your garden, water has an indefinable appeal that can only be summarized crudely by the bland word 'interest'. Time seems to fly by when you sit by water and half an hour can pass as if in an instant because a well-planned pool contains not only the plants, fish and snails that you have put there but also myriads of other creatures, attracted as magnetically to the presence of the water as we are. Insect life abounds below, on and above the water surface and can range from beetles, pond skaters and caddis larvae to dragonflies. Amphibians will almost inevitably arrive, as if by magic – frogs, toads and newts will lay their spawn and bird life too will seek out the water of your pool, especially if you can keep a small area free from ice in the winter; although one always hopes the local heron population isn't among them.

You can't simply put a water feature anywhere that takes your fancy and expect it to be attractive and function properly. Like soil, water is a highly dynamic medium, an inorganic chemical matrix within which are a huge number of organic ingredients, most of them living. I have often thought the distinction between soil and water is not nearly as clear-cut as most people seem to imagine. At a scientific conference on water fungi a few years ago, I gave a paper entitled 'Soil as an Aquatic Medium' and even surprised my colleagues. For water is one of the most important components of soil, and soil

Positioning of a pond is critical if it is to be successful. This pool is rather too close to the overhanging trees.

is one of the most important components of many aquatic habits, certainly those in gardens. Just as you can squeeze water from a fistful of garden soil, so you will probably scoop up plenty of soil from the bottom of your garden pond.

The siting of a water feature, especially a pond, is critical. The position should have as close as possible to eight hours of direct illumination each day. It's sometimes suggested or implied that this must apply to the whole surface area of the pond but this isn't necessary – half or even a third of the surface area with full exposure to the sky is adequate, especially if there is some water movement. And its size? Self-contained water features will fit into the smallest of spaces and truly tiny pools can be constructed but the larger the pool, the easier it is to maintain a viable balance between water, plants and animal life. My experience has been that the minimum effective size for an outdoor garden pool is about 1.5 x 1.2m/ 5 x 4ft with a depth of at least 30cm/12in although

my warm greenhouse pool is smaller than this and so-called tub gardens are smaller still. My wildlife pond, which functions extremely well is irregular in shape but has a total area of approximately 28m²/300 square feet, the deep end is 1m/3¼ft, shallowing to 60cm/24in over the rest of the area but with a 20–25cm/8–10in deep ledge all the way round and wider at certain places than others.

CONSTRUCTION

The modern pond in the modern garden is usually and best constructed by using a butyl 'rubber' liner. Puddled clay and concrete linings are largely things of the past and whilst pre-formed plastic liners (rather like large, irregular baby's baths) are widely available and easy to install, they are impractical for large pools, constrain you to a pre-determined shape and depth and aren't easy to disguise. For most gardeners, therefore, I recommend butyl rubber and you will find instructions and illustrations showing you how to excavate a pond and fit a liner in many gardening books. When I see these, I am often reminded of the wonderful question I was asked on *Gardeners' Question Time* some years ago. A man had read up on the subject of double digging but wanted to know why, when he did it, the soil didn't come out of the ground in neat cubes labelled A, B and C. Yes, I fear that pond instructions are sometimes self-evidently written by people who have never done it so I will take a moment to give some common sense advice based on my own experiences.

Don't economize on your choice of liner. Buy the best you can afford, as there must be few things more frustrating than finding your newly established pool has sprung a leak because you bought a thin or otherwise inferior liner. And do shop around. Pond liners vary principally in the thickness of the butyl rubber sheet but they are often priced according to the length of the guarantee, which can vary from about five years to 'a lifetime'. I've always been slightly unsure of what this means. If a ten-year old child buys a pond liner as a ninety-fifth birthday present for his great-grandfather, whose lifetime governs the length of the guarantee? And something I have recently been told makes me even more wary. I am informed that in order to out-do each other, some manufacturers have been extending the length of the guarantee without in any way changing the specification of the product. What you could buy five years ago with a ten-year guarantee, you can now buy 'badge engineered' with a twenty-five-year or even longer guarantee and, most importantly, costs more in consequence. My advice is to go to a reputable, unbiased retailer, look at thickness rather than longevity and take the expert's guidance.

Much foolish advice has been written about the installation of pond liners. No matter how thick it is, a liner can be punctured by sharp objects so some form of underlay is desirable to give protection from flints or debris in the soil; no matter how carefully you check the inside of the

hole, small things can still be missed. Placing the liner on a layer of sand is often suggested – but I can only conclude suggested by people who have never tried laying sand down the vertical sides of a hole. In any event, in a garden where the water table may be fairly near the surface during heavy winter rain, sand will very soon dissipate from beneath the liner and the protection will quite literally drain away. A commonly suggested alternative is old carpet. If the carpet is polypropylene or other plastic and very flexible, it might succeed. If it contains any wool or other natural fibre, it won't, because the structure will be lost as the natural material slowly rots. There is no effective and reliable alternative to purpose-made

ABOVE LEFT: My wildlife pond has ledges and a deeper area where fish and other animals spend the winter. ABOVE RIGHT: A double layer of fabric underlay is essential if the liner isn't to be punctured by sharp stones or other debris.

proprietary fleece underlay. It is easy to handle, flexible and durable and I always use it in a double layer. Having placed underlay and liner in place with plenty of overlap at the sides, slowly fill the pond with a hose. The liner will take up the strain and stretch to fit the hole as you do so although I find it helps to ease it into place with a soft broom. At first, you will probably be pretty horrified at the unashamedly artificial and look nothing remotely like the lovely water feature you saw in your mind's eye. Banish these concerns. Black pond liners 'disappear' within a year due to the overgrowth of algae and the encrustations of limo deposits from the water. In truth, the liner in my wild life pond, folds and all, is now almost indistinguishable from submerged rocks.

WATER MOVEMENT

I've come to the conclusion that adequate oxygenation is the biggest key to the success of garden ponds. And I've also come to the conclusion

that this is achieved much the most easily by movement of the water. Like most other gardeners, I read and was told that the way to oxygenate water is 'the natural way' – by using oxygenators. These are more or less totally submerged plants that, like other green vegetation, give off oxygen through their leaves. Instead of this dissipating into the atmosphere as it does with terrestrial species, the oxygen passes into the water to help create a suitable environment for fish, other forms of aquatic life and other plants. It's a good theory but it just doesn't work in practice. I haven't seen the calculations, but self-evidently there isn't enough oxygen. And in any event, I don't believe it is the natural way. I challenge anybody to find a natural expanse of water where there is vigorous aquatic life, none of the foul smells that are symptomatic of anaerobic decay – and no water movement. Rivers

The liner stretches under the weight of the water and the black shiny appearance rapidly vanishes as algae start to grow over it.

and streams patently have water movement for oxygenation, lakes have streams running into and out of them; so do many ponds, even if the flow is in a culvert or below the surface and not immediately apparent. Occasionally you will find a totally isolated pond with no water flow either in or out, and apparently healthy; but it is usually so utterly choked with aquatic vegetation that it is scarcely a thing of beauty and any fish or other aquatic life are all but invisible. So if it won't do in nature, it won't do in gardens. If you want submerged, oxygenating plants in your pond, have them by all means, but rely on them totally and you will have a pond that will be probably be of neither use nor ornament. The maxim for a healthy, vigorous garden pond is to ensure that it is oxygenated because the water moves, and preferably moves all year round.

Water movement in a formal pond is achieved most commonly and easily with some type of fountain. Air is dragged into the water as it splashes back and so the pond is agitated and simply and efficiently oxygenated. The fountain, or at least the jet from it, is nonetheless often far too big and both visually and functionally wrong. It's easy to over-cool the water, especially in a small pond, by setting the fountain jet too high, too wide or simply by having too many of them – rather like the rose on a watering can. There's nothing clever about trying to emulate Trafalgar Square. (And don't forget that water lilies, the cream of many people's ponds, don't thrive in water that has too much movement or with cold water being sprayed constantly on to their leaves. Keep them away from the fountain and ensure the fountain itself is not set too high).

When choosing your fountain, you need not stick to what the manufacturers think you should have. With the assured safety of a low-voltage system, why not adapt it to your needs? Many years ago I bought at auction a small, late-eighteenth or early-nineteenth-century lead fountain head. It is essentially a hollow urn-shaped structure with lions' heads on either side. It was (relatively) simple to mount it on a small modern pump such that the fountain outlet tube constantly spurts water upwards into the sphere from where it then cascades out of the lion's mouths by courtesy of gravity. It looks perfect on my small lily pond, where anything modern would have been totally out of place.

In the monthly calendar of hints in many old, and some not so old, gardening books is the late-autumn advice to clean out the fountain pump and put it away for the winter. I do no such thing,

A pond without water movement may be all right for a farm field, but really isn't satisfactory for a garden.

largely because even with the relatively mild winters that seem to have become the norm, hard frosts still occur at least a few times each year in most districts and ponds will freeze if the water is still. Clean out your fountain pump in autumn by all means, but then put it back in the pond, not in the garden shed. In all but the hardest frosts, an area of water will remain unfrozen so any gases from decomposing matter in the pond can escape, oxygen can enter and, most importantly, local birds will be guaranteed somewhere to drink.

Modern fountain pumps are nothing if not versatile and, by swapping connectors and hoses, can as readily be used to power waterfalls and streams. But be careful. An artificial stream is perhaps the hardest of all garden features to create. More often than not they look frankly stupid; they look stupid largely because they begin and end where a real stream couldn't or

In a formal pond, close to a house, a classical fountain is perfectly appropriate; in a wildlife pond it would look frankly ridiculous.

wouldn't. Yet again, my advice is to look first at the way nature does it and see how real streams function. I grant that it's unreasonable to expect a convenient hillside down which your stream can tumble, or a river into which it can flow, but small streams usually start life as a spring bubbling from a hole in the ground and this is relatively easy to create in a way that looks both realistic and attractive. I like to place large stones around the hole entrance and to part-conceal it at the foot of a hedge or by a path-side. Because an artificial stream, unlike a natural one, must of necessity have recirculating water, the simplest and most convincing outlet for your stream should be in a pond from which a submerged pump returns it, through a buried pipe, to your starting hole.

Another reason why artificial streams so often fail visually is the difficulty of concealing the plastic liner. Unlike the more or less still water of a pond, the running water of a stream will soon displace pebbles or gravel used to conceal the sheet unless they are embedded in mortar. This can be done but remember too that such a 'river bed' must be constructed carefully to look authentic because the stones themselves will not be mellowed by algal growth and other sediments as happens in a pond. Look at some natural streams first and see the way the pebbles are arranged in them before attempting to mimic it. (Generally speaking, the large pebbles are in the middle, grading to small ones at the sides.) Use a mortar base like an aquatic glue to hold everything in place.

WATER PLANTS

One of the basics that any prospective water gardener learns is that plants for the water garden fall into a number of distinct categories which require significantly different treatments, in effect depending on how great is their demand for an aquatic environment. What isn't always apparent is that even within these categories, there are some important variations.

At one extreme are submerged plants, which live entirely or almost entirely underwater, sometimes hardly even rooted in the pool mud and rising above the water surface, if at all, only to flower. They might be thought scarcely worthy of cultivation but in fact they are among the most important pool plants, especially in a semi-natural or informal pool. I have already shot some holes in the conventional wisdom that they are valuable in oxygenating the water but that isn't to diminish their importance. To my mind, their more useful role is in providing spawning places for fish and amphibians and hiding places and shelter for other aquatic life. One big and unavoidable problem associated with submerged plants, however, is that they also form a most effective substrate on which blanket weed thrives. (I have yet to find a better or more effective way of limiting blanket weed growth than by regularly netting it with a strong and robust net on a

telescopic handle. In recent years, thanks to climate change, you will have found me even having to do this in mid-winter, something that only a few years ago would have been unimaginable.)

Unfortunately, many species of exotic submerged plants are highly invasive and have been grown in garden ponds or other ornamental water gardens with the best of intentions but have since become naturalized in the wider environment and caused considerable damage to native vegetation. Historically, the most troublesome species in Britain was the Canadian pondweed (*Elodea canadensis*). When it was first introduced here in the early

The most attractive of submerged plants is water crowfoot, often seen for sale at garden centres, but it is a species for running water, not your garden pond.

nineteenth century – not into garden ponds but into canals, slow moving rivers and similar habitats – it proved to be extremely invasive and blocked navigation channels. You will still see Canadian pondweed for sale at your local garden centre and this is because, over the years, it has quietened down. The explanation is believed to be that the original introduction was of a vigorous male clone. The form now sold for garden and aquarium use is female and much more restrained in its growth although I still don't think it is a plant to turn your back on for long. There are other species of *Elodea* but they too have recently begun to spread aggressively and, in the unlikely event of your seeing them for sale, resist the temptation to buy. The most aggressive of all oxygenators are the New Zealand pygmyweed (*Crassula helmsii*, also sometimes called *Tillaea recurva*) and the South American parrot's feather (*Myriophyllum aquaticum*, also called *M. brasiliense*) the planting of which is officially discouraged. Considerable publicity has been given recently to the problems of alien vegetation invading natural habitats so, even if they are still to be found for sale, they should be avoided like the plague.

To my mind, the most seductively lovely of submerged plants is the native water crowfoot (*Ranunculus aquatilis*), a white-flowered water buttercup with grass-like submerged leaves and celery-like floating ones. It is widely offered for sale but will almost invariably disappoint because its true habitat is not the still or rippled water of your pond but the fast flowing, clear current of natural streams, its roots anchoring it to the bed with astonishing tenacity. I have yet to satisfy myself as to how newly emerged seedlings achieve their initial foothold in what is often a torrential flow.

Floating plants are those that have either no roots or roots that dangle into the water but none are anchored in any way. They die down in the winter to survive as dormant buds, resting in the mud of the pool floor to grow and rise again with the arrival of warmer conditions in the spring. Like some submerged plants, many species of floating plant multiply vegetatively with great rapidity and in consequence can cause serious problems if they are allowed into rivers, canals or other water courses. For this reason, the sale of species such as water hyacinth (*Eichhornia crassipes*) may be restricted in some areas, especially those with warmer climates, such as parts of the southern United States where the winter offers less of a check to their development. In Britain, the commonest floating plants are the North American floating fern known as fairy moss (*Azolla filiculoides*) and one or other of our three native species of duckweed (*Lemna*). *Azolla* is a beautiful thing as its tiny fronds change from green to red in autumn but it too falls into the category of invasive aliens and sadly I have to advise you to avoid growing it – if you can. It arrived recently in my

*The lovely water hyacinth (*Eichhornia crassipes*) is one of a number of aquatic plants which can cause havoc if they escape into the wild.*

own wildlife pond courtesy of the feet of a visiting mallard. In such a small area, nothing regularly keeps it in check, but it's perhaps worth adding that a recent government report estimated the cost of eradicating *Azolla* from two hundred sites in which it had become established at between £200,000 and £2,000,000 over a three- to five-year period. Comparable or even higher figures have been calculated for the likes of *Crassula helmsii* and *Myriophyllum aquaticum*. I think I am in a significant minority, however, in welcoming duckweed in my pond – at least, in my native plant pond. There, it looks attractive, provides shade and shelter for aquatic creatures and can be contained by frequent netting. In my formal pond, it would look out of place and I rigorously remove any small patches I see – they arrive unannounced and uninvited on birds' feet.

The group I call basic water plants are those that grow within the pool, anchored in the mud but with leaves and flowers arising to float at the surface or be raised above it. It is a large and diverse group including the tall, angular spiky burr reed (*Sparganium erectum*), the blue-flowered pickerel weed (*Pontederia cordata*) with its arrow-head leaves, the fragrantly scented water hawthorn (*Aponogeton distachyos*) and my long-time favourite, the aquatic aroid called golden club (*Orontium aquaticum*) with its candle-like flower spikes. All are best and most conveniently planted in purpose-made planting baskets. But the classic water plants are water lilies. They have traditionally

been expensive for reasons that I don't fully understand, as by and large they are not difficult to propagate – hacking a piece off the rootstock with an axe is usually sufficient. I suspect the reason may be a combination of it only being possible to obtain rather few individuals from each rootstock and the fact that rather few nurseries grow them so demand always exceeds supply. Someone seems to have cracked the problem, nonetheless, as some supermarkets are now selling very modestly priced water lilies each spring alongside their house plants and bunches of chrysanthemums.

Sadly, most of those I have seen don't come equipped with as much detail about planting depth and pool size as I would like. This is unfortunate because water lilies exemplify one of the most important features of the water plant group, in that the depth of water to which they are most suited and the vigour of their surface spread varies considerably between varieties. They must therefore be chosen carefully because there are few gardening experiences more frustrating than discovering that, just when your water lily has established itself, the entire surface of the pool is vanishing beneath its all-covering carpet of foliage. For instance, given a hankering for a white-flowered water lily, you have a choice from something like *Nymphaea* 'Albatros', which requires a water depth of about 10–30cm/4–12in and has a surface spread of up to 30cm/12in, to our native *N. alba*, tolerant of water from 1–2m/3¼–6½ft depth and spreading up to 2m/6½ft across with gigantic leaves. Sadly, because water lily nurseries and suppliers are rather sparse, people appear to be too easily seduced by what is available. Even good and otherwise tasteful gardeners seem to throw discernment aside when making their selection and I have seen the most lovely of pools in the most beautiful and carefully designed of gardens sprouting a highly inappropriate rainbow mixture of water lily flowers. (I think there may also be something of the same misplaced flair that makes brightly coloured clothes – such as Hawaiian shirts – look so appealing when you buy them on holiday in a hot climate but which look frankly dreadful when you get them home.)

So you may have to hunt rather widely to find exactly the combination of colour and vigour you want. I hope however you don't have quite the difficulty I experienced when planting the warm pool in my greenhouse. The pool is tiny and I wanted a tiny tropical water lily for it. And I reason that if you are having a tropical water lily, it should be of a colour unobtainable in hardy lilies – blue or close to it. My knowledge and researches indicated only one tiny, blue flowered water lily variety, 'August Koch'. But because tropical water lilies are rarely grown in Britain, no British nursery had one. Nor did any elsewhere in Europe and I was obliged to have it express air-freighted from Florida at appalling cost. Nonetheless, it arrived in pristine condition twenty-four hours after leaving its birthplace, has graced my greenhouse ever since, is hardly out of

flower all summer long and I don't begrudge a cent of the price. I should perhaps add in passing that an indoor pool, whatever its size, almost always benefits from some additional heating. The normal water temperature in my greenhouse is about two degrees below the ambient air temperature, which is set to a year-round minimum of 13°C/55°F. This is insufficient for tropical water lilies (and tropical fish), which require a minimum of about 20°C/68°F, so I have a submerged aquarium heater to make up the difference.

Like other pond plants, water lilies are usually planted in one of two ways – in pockets or ledges constructed at the edges of the pond when the thing is being built, or in plastic baskets placed in the water. There are occasions however when neither is ideal. In my small formal lily pond, there are no planting pockets and in any event I want the lilies to be growing away from the edge in open water. I could of course use large planting baskets but the water is clear for much of the year and I'm afraid that, functionally effective though they may be, I don't find large plastic baskets to be especially attractive features. They seem little improvement on the archetypal village pond's discarded supermarket trolley. My solution is to use

PAGE 112: Nymphaea 'Marliacea Albida' is an ideal white-flowered water lily for a small pond, as it isn't too vigorous. PAGE 113: Nymphaea 'August Koch', one of the very few non-vigorous blue water lilies in the tiny warm-water pond in my greenhouse.

large plain terracotta pots filled with aquatic plant compost and carefully submerged. They soon become covered with green algal growth, are perfectly attractive when seen through the clear water, even in winter when the plants are dormant, and they don't appear to deteriorate in any significant way.

Plants that grow at the edge of the water are called marginals. The group covers a range of habitat requirements from those species like bog bean (*Menyanthes trifoliata*) – a spreading, almost scrambling plant with large, three-lobed, broad bean-like leaves and small white, star-like flowers, that must exist permanently in a few centimetres of water – through those like arrowhead (*Sagittaria sagittifolia*) – that tolerate periodic drying out of the water's edge – to those like the beautiful giant 'buttercup', the marsh marigold (*Caltha palustris*) – that need really saturated, waterlogged soil but preferably not standing water. Because marginal plants come into such intimate contact with the pool liner (which is likely to be butyl rubber sheet), particular care is needed both in their selection and their planting. Some marginal plants have strongly growing, invasive and, most importantly, sharp rhizomes that will readily puncture the sheet and initiate a leak. Top of the list of those to avoid are the several species of reedmace (*Typha*), sometimes popularly called bulrushes, which are in any event far too vigorous for most small pools but which have needle-like rhizome tips.

WATER WILDLIFE

There is a degree of overlap between marginal plants and bog garden plants but before I leave the garden pond and discuss bog gardening, it's important I say something about animal life in the pond as there may be legal implications here, as there is with invasive pond plants. Frogs, toads and newts will probably arrive in your pond to breed, especially if there is plenty of plant life. If they don't, there isn't much you can do about it.

*Marsh marigold (*Caltha palustris*), one of the classic native marginal species.*

Because of the risk of spreading red leg disease, frogs mustn't be transferred from wild ponds into garden ponds and, by a similar token, nor should any animals or excess frog spawn be taken in the opposite direction. By moving animals into an unsuitable habitat, you could even be committing an offence under a little-appreciated but important piece of legislation, the Abandonment of Animals Act 1960. It's essential, moreover, to have pond edges that enable amphibians to escape. Formal ponds with overhanging slabs are particularly hazardous – it isn't generally appreciated that amphibians can drown.

I think a good deal of nonsense is said and written about snails in ponds. It is commonly asserted that snails are essential 'to keep the pond clean' by consuming algae, fish faeces and the like, and that accordingly you should buy some. I have never bought pond snails and my ponds are full of them. They arrive on water plants and as eggs attached to birds' feet. I am sure they are an important part of the aquatic ecosystem. But in my experience, they don't make the slightest difference to the clarity, appearance or general health of the water.

Most pond owners will want to stock their pond with ornamental fish – generally goldfish in one or other of their varied forms, or the lovely golden orfe. They are excellent and easy to care for. Unless you are serious about your fish keeping, I would steer you away from being seduced into buying koi carp, which may be extremely beautiful but are also extremely expensive and require careful attention of the kind not usually met in a normal garden pond. Other types of fish are also commonly encountered at garden centres but most are pretty unsuitable. Golden rudd are fairly attractive and easy to keep but golden tench, once in the pond, will seldom be seen – they are bottom-living fish and will simply churn up the mud. Immature sterlets (*Acipenser ruthenus*), a species of sturgeon, are also sometimes seen for sale – don't be unwise enough to buy them. They too are bottom-living so you will never see them and, in the unlikely event of them surviving, they will soon outgrow their space.

If you have a wildlife pond, you may wish to populate it, as I have, with native fish species. Here too, choose carefully. Small to medium sized fish, appropriate to pond rather than river life and not permanently bottom-living are appropriate. In my own pond I have minnows (*Phoxinus phoxinus*), three-spined sticklebacks (*Gasterosteus aculeatus*) and rudd (*Scardinus erythrophthalmus*); they are all most successful and breed. Such species can generally be obtained (often to special order) from specialist aquatic suppliers. If you want to net a few fry from your nearest river or lake, you will need permission from the landowner and the owner of the fishing rights and also a permit from the Environment Agency under the Salmon and Freshwater Fisheries Act 1975.

BOG GARDENS

The bog garden is the most varied of all water garden habitats. It is a curiosity that while water features in gardens have never been more popular, their slightly drier companions, bog gardens, seem paradoxically to have missed the boat. I am unsure why this should be, as a bog garden is much easier to create than a pond (there's no need to worry about leaks) and the range of plants that can be grown there is much greater and satisfyingly different from those of conventional 'dry land' beds and borders. Perhaps it is simply the less than appealing name itself. 'Bog garden' doesn't conjure up an immediately endearing vision although no-one seems to have produced anything better.

At one extreme in the bog garden are the plants only one step removed from the marginals themselves, which need extremely wet soil. They are what I might usefully call conventional bog garden species – plants such as marsh cinquefoil (*Potentilla palustris*), Himalayan cowslip (*Primula florindae*), water avens (*Geum rivale*), *Rodgersia* and the globe flowers (*Trollius*). At the other end of the spectrum are those species requiring moisture retentive soil but which are intolerant of real waterlogging. Many of them never receive a mention in most water gardening books as they are considered merely border perennials but I believe the more informal type of water garden that include a bog garden, should grade gradually into the other, drier parts of the remainder. Among

the more unexpected bog garden plants I have in mind are such perennials as bugle (*Ajuga reptans*), elephant's ears (*Bergenia*), dusky cranesbill (*Geranium phaeum*), day lily (*Hemerocallis*), snowflakes (*Leucojum*), catchfly (*Lychnis chalcedonica*) and New Zealand flax (*Phormium*).

But if bog gardens and bog plants in general don't receive the attention and interest they really merit, there is one group of plants that is all but ignored. How often do you hear of a bog shrub or a bog tree? Yet walk alongside any river, stream, pond or other natural water course and you will almost invariably be in the company of at least some woody plants. It's true that not many waterside trees are suitable for gardens, partly because most grow rather tall but mainly because the quantity of deposited foliage (even from evergreens) will be more than the volume of water can absorb without being fouled. But small wetland shrubs are another matter and I find them especially valuable in providing height in the bog garden and close to the water's edge, particularly in winter.

In passing, I should add that the obvious way to achieve this all-year round 'vertical interest' in

PAGE 116–17: Frogs will find their way to your pond naturally, and are increasingly reliant on gardens as farm ponds become polluted. RIGHT: Bog gardens don't have to accompany ponds. This one is in a permanently wet hollow in a garden with very heavy soil.

informal or semi-natural water gardens is with some of the medium-height clump-forming sedges such as *Cyperus* or hop sedge (*Carex pseudocyperus*). Sedges shouldn't be cut back in winter in the way that many grasses are because they won't regenerate as successfully from the base.

Among the best of the bog garden shrubs are willows, but certainly not the tree-sized weeping willow (*Salix* x *sepulcralis 'Chrysocoma'*), which is far too big and far too fond of drains, nor the so-called alpine or dwarf willows like *S. lanata* or *S. repens*, which are intolerant of the moisture-laden atmosphere. Best are those species with attractively coloured bark, such as *S. alba subsp. vitellina* 'Britzensis', also called 'Chermesina', with orange-red winter bark colour, and *S. daphnoides*, with purple shoots and white powdery bloom. These may be cut back hard in spring to limit their size and ensure a regular supply of brightly coloured young stems, in much the same way as

with the coloured-stemmed dogwoods (*Cornus*). If your soil is acidic, or can be satisfactorily acidified, then try bog rosemary (*Andromeda polifolia*), bog myrtle (*Myrica gale*) or, in strongly acid conditions, even species of *Vaccinium* like cowberry (*V. vitis-idaea*), *V. delavayi*, *V. glaucoalbum* or *V. nummularia*.

Having said that leaking isn't a concern with bog gardens, I should perhaps pass on a hint about how they can be constructed simply. The need is for an area of soil that is permanently wet but not too wet – I sometimes remind gardeners of the difference between a bog and a swamp. By my definition, a bog has more soil than water, a swamp the reverse. On a heavy soil in a region of high rainfall and a natural or artificially dug hollow (especially at the foot of a slope), such a thing may arise naturally. Nonetheless, even here it can't be relied on to stay permanently wet enough, especially with the increased frequency of warm and dry summers that climate change promises. With my light soil, more or less flat garden and our fairly low rainfall, it would be even more chancy. The answer is to dig out a hollow, exactly as you might for a pond but of 30cm/12in or at most 45cm/18in depth. Line it with the cheapest pond liner you can obtain (or, at a pinch, even old plastic bags) and punch some holes in it. Before backfilling, you need to ensure as much continuity

*Bog shrubs are a little-appreciated and little-grown group of species. This is the native bog myrtle (*Myrica gale*).*

of water supply as possible and I achieve this by channeling the rainwater from the greenhouse and other nearby garden buildings through pipes laid in shallow trenches. The outlet of the pipes should be placed in a pocket of coarse gravel (to prevent soil from blocking the end) and then the hole is re-filled, adding a quantity of organic matter as you do so.

OTHER WATER FEATURES

There is one highly important aspect to water gardening that simply can't be avoided. It is something that really applies to no other aspect of gardening and was recently brought home to me when a four-year-old child, momentarily unsupervized at a playgroup in a neighbouring village, wandered into an adjoining garden to be found, but minutes later, tragically drowned in the pond. Garden ponds and young children simply don't mix. It is wholly unrealistic to expect any parent to watch their infants continuously, just as it is aesthetically unsatisfactory to have a garden pond and yet keep it permanently netted. I am unrepentant in my view that an existing pond in a garden where young children live should be filled in until they are older, and new ones not constructed. The existing pond needn't be uprooted but can easily and quickly be converted into a bog garden. But as I have already emphasized, the movement and sound of water is particularly attractive and no bog garden will provide this. The answer is to install one of the many creations that have come to be known as 'water features'.

These include wall fountains, in which water spills either from an amorphous spout or something like the mouth of an imitation classical mask. They can be both effective and attractive, but bear in mind that they can't be attached to the wall of your house or to a garden boundary wall (without very obliging neighbours) because, while the spout is fixed attractively to one side of the wall, the pump and other attachments are best placed on the other. And never underestimate how annoying it can be to hear the constant sound of water trickling on the other side of a boundary wall. Perhaps simplest and most versatile are so-called bubble or pebble fountains – small ground features such as piles of pebbles or single pieces of rock (slate 'monoliths' are currently in vogue and they can look lovely), out of which or over which water trickles. They can be constructed piecemeal from a small fountain pump but purpose-made kits are now available comprising, in effect, a tiny plastic pond complete with pump which is placed in a hole in the ground and then filled with rocks, pebbles or whatever takes your fancy. It's probably fair to say that with modern technology and ingenuity, no garden is too small for a water feature of some sort; and rightly so.

I am fortunate to have an old well in my garden which I have made the centre of an attractive feature.

WILDLIFE
GARDENING

WILDLIFE GARDENING

It was many years before I had my first purpose-made wildlife garden. I stress purpose-made because every garden contains wildlife. Anything living you haven't personally placed there is wildlife by definition, albeit often unwelcome – I doubt if anyone has ever created a garden deliberately to attract aphids, slugs and woodlice. The reason for the absence of a wildlife garden from my portfolio was nothing to do with a lack of interest in the subject; far from it. I was a naturalist before I was a gardener and have always believed my gardening knowledge and interest grew from that early passion. But the notion of recreating a small portion of the wild world close to your home, of managing it for your own pleasure and satisfaction, and most especially of growing plants in it that are natives is rather recent. I can remember the gardening page of a national tabloid newspaper as recently as fifteen or so years ago when John Chambers, owner of one of the first of the serious native plant nurseries, issued his seed catalogue. 'Weeds for Sale' was the banner. And that was essentially most gardeners' reaction. It was a reaction that was tempered when, in the late 1980s, he first displayed wildflowers at the Chelsea Flower Show and from 1990, when designer Julie Toll began to stage gardens there in which native plants took the dominant role. It was tempered even more when she won Gold Medals with them. The attitude hasn't completely gone away, however, especially among gardeners of the older generation, but overall the atmosphere has undoubtedly changed.

IMPACT ON THE ENVIRONMENT

Wildlife or native plant gardening is part of the wider concern for the environment that has developed gradually over the past thirty or forty years. It's a trend that has spread well beyond amateur gardeners and while many local councils were once rightly vilified for spraying roadside verges with weed killer, the highway authorities now buy native flower seeds at considerable expense for the mass sowing of motorway embankments. As with much of the modern environmental movement, a pedigree can be traced back to 1962 when the American writer Rachel Carson published her profoundly disturbing book *Silent Spring*. Much of her concern centred on the widespread use of persistent pesticides with damaging side-effects. But it is only a short step from the concern about organochlorine insecticides causing the deaths of birds of prey to the posing of questions about almost every other human interference with the natural environment. So it came to be recognized that the increasing scarcity of many once-familiar wildflowers could be fairly reasonably explained. It was attributable to an increase in the use of herbicides by farmers and others and to the destruction of more and more of their natural habitats, partly by agricultural and forestry activity but also because of the encroachment of

Umbelliferous plants are among the most important wildlife species for early summer.

urban areas and motorways into what had once been countryside.

Gradually, it was realized that it is in most cases impossible to turn back the clock and replace what has disappeared, so some gardeners felt that they could play a helpful part by growing wildflowers in their gardens. This was an understandable but misguided sentiment. The growing of wildflowers, even rare wildflowers, in gardens is unlikely to make much impact on their long-term survival. They will still be rare in the wild and none of us is likely to grow species that would become extinct without our intervention. You simply cannot *create* a natural, or even a semi-natural, habitat in your garden. What you see 'in the wild', to use a popular phrase, is the result of many years – in some instances many hundreds or even thousands of years – of gradual ecological development, a community of plants and animals whose composition is constantly shifting until eventually it reaches a more or less stable state called a climax. You might be able to create something that looks superficially similar and that gives huge satisfaction and pleasure. But neither your wildlife garden nor a motorway verge seeded with native plants comes close to being the real thing. What it can do, apart from giving you much pleasure, is to provide a haven and food source for many species of wild animal. So although it won't 'save the planet' and, paradoxically, will do little for the good of our native vegetation, it can be of much benefit to our native animals.

PREPARING THE WILDLIFE GARDEN

Anyone who begins to cultivate native plants, especially in a small garden, will soon discover that many of them present problems – the problems that have caused horticulturists in the past to reject or selectively breed from them to produce plants more appropriate for gardening. First, most native plants have fairly short flowering seasons and in a small area it is difficult to grow a large enough range to provide interest all year round. Second, many native plants are remarkably invasive, especially when grown in a garden away from their natural competitors. I am astonished to see that seeds of ground elder, bindweed and hairy bittercress are offered for sale with no warning of their potential. A plot of native plants requires careful management. If you leave it to its own devices, you will have not a wild garden but a wilderness.

My own native plant/wildlife garden has been developed over the past few years and it has taught me much about the pitfalls and keys to success. You won't be able to follow precisely my blueprint because everyone's space and time commitments are different but I hope it will give you guidelines and a basic plan of action.

The area I have committed to the wildlife garden is approximately 175m²/200 square yards, which I think is about ideal. If the area is smaller than this, you will find many of the plants are just too vigorous for the whole ever to look really attractive; if the area is much bigger, rather different management considerations apply and it becomes unworkable. My plot is a recent addition purchased from a neighbour and had been a long-neglected cottage garden – we had to begin by removing several skipfuls of domestic rubbish. The vegetation comprised a tangle of well-established creeping buttercup, field bindweed, stinging nettles, sow-thistles, lesser celandine and dandelion together with substantial populations of groundsel, shepherd's purse, hairy bitter cress, several species of speedwell and other weeds of cultivation. There was a crude boundary of long-dead elms, the victims of elm disease several years earlier and a few rather untidy old Lawson cypresses. Unpromising? Not at all – almost ideal.

The most important feature was that the area had been neglected so the soil lacked any artificial fertilizer. Trying to develop a garden of native plants on a vegetable plot or other recently cultivated area is frustrating because the fertilizer will encourage lush vegetative growth, especially of grasses, at the expense of flowers. If there is no alternative to such an area, it is worth first sowing one or more crops of a vegetable that has a high nitrogen demand, like a brassica, on the plot. Space the plants closely (don't of course give any more fertilizer) and then remove all the plant matter at the end of the season. The one other way to weaken grass growth is deliberately to augment the grass seed mixture with semi-parasitic plants – yellow rattle (*Rhinanthus minor*) is the most

readily obtained – which will depress the vigour of some of the more aggressive species.

It's true that most of the existing plants fell into my category of invasive garden weeds but their removal really presented no problem because I don't subscribe to the view that all chemical use in a garden is wrong. Use of the translocated weed killer glyphosate (see page 22) is the only effective way to eradicate the bulk of the existing weed growth and it will not persist in the soil. Once it had done its job, no chemical would be used in the area ever again but without it we couldn't even have started. The presence of this tangle of old vegetation meant there would already be a large population of animal life, mostly small and invertebrate but also including voles and mice – essential inhabitants of a wildlife area, although perhaps less welcome in a conventional garden.

Whatever the condition of the site, you will need to allow 12–18 months for one reason or another before you begin to see something resembling a native plant garden. So a measure of patience is necessary. In the first winter on our plot, we felled the old elms and ground out the stumps – an essential precaution whenever broad-leaved trees are cut down but one that is often overlooked. Time and again I hear of gardeners who decide to 'grow a clematis' over a felled stump, an unwise course because it is through the cut surfaces of the stumps of broad-leaved trees that honey fungus (*Armillaria mellea*) most readily enters and becomes established in a garden. I left the cypresses after tidying them up. They are the only non-native plants in the wildlife garden but they justifiy their presence by providing valuable cover and screening.

We also dug the wildlife pond in the first winter. I have already said much about water gardens in general in the previous chapter and will describe the planting of this one later. As the winter was extremely wet, ground water constantly appeared in the base of the hole and we weren't able to lay the liner until the following spring. The summer, however, was fortunately fairly hot and dry and we used it to eradicate the existing weeds. We sprayed five times in total with a glyphosate-containing weed killer. I am regularly told that gardeners have used glyphosate (often following my recommendation) and that it doesn't work. It does, and will eradicate most weeds except horsetail and Japanese knotweed. Firstly, it is essential to spray in hot, dry conditions (the official recommendation is that there must be six hours without rain after application in order for it to work properly) and secondly, you must repeat it at least twice. Every two weeks is necessary with most deep-rooted perennial weeds. After about seven days, the weeds stop growing. About seven days later, they begin to show signs of yellowing. That is the cue to spray again. By late summer, the area was relatively free of vegetation. A few more spot treatments of the sow-thistles, which proved surprisingly more difficult to eradicate than the bindweed, and I felt happy I could safely rotovate in preparation for sowing. It's important to sow before early autumn if possible.

BELOW LEFT: My own wildlife garden as we began to clear it for sowing. Some fastigiate trees are already in place. BELOW: An infrastructure of stepping stones and the old farm trough are in place before sowing. RIGHT: The original flora of my wildlife garden might look attractive, but it is largely composed of invasive and inappropriate species.

THE WILDFLOWER MEADOW

There is a big difference between the appearance of a native plant garden in winter, or when it is first sown, and in early summer. Your 'meadow' will then be a metre or more in height and you won't be able to stroll through it and enjoy the plants unless you make pathways. This can be done informally, simply by regularly mowing strips across it, but I took the more permanent course of laying stepping stone paths across the whole area as soon as the ground had settled after rotavating. There are several advantages to this. They serve to divide the area into segments, in which I was able to sow slightly different seed mixtures (accepting that over time, the boundaries would blur as seed was set and dispersed from one segment to the other). They also allow access close to the pond for viewing without any risk of the pond edge being damaged or collapsed. And of course they mean the pathways don't become unacceptably muddy even in wet weather.

There are essentially three approaches to the creation of an area of native plants. You can sow or plant entirely piecemeal using individual plants or species, you can sow or plant individual species into an overall sowing of wild grasses or you can use a 'wildflower' seed mixture containing both grasses and wildflowers. My experience is that the latter two are the better courses but that you must be prepared to adjust, adapt and modify. Several seed firms now specialize in selling seed mixtures, with greater or lesser details of exactly what each

contains. Typically, they are called meadow mixtures, wildflower mixtures, woodland mixtures, pond-edge mixtures and so on. The biggest drawback to the ready-made mixtures is that they may well not contain your favourite wildflower, the suppliers may not describe which grasses they include and they often contain too much ox-eye daisy. I have no real objection to ox-eye daisy, even considerable quantities of ox-eye daisy, in meadow or even hedgerow mixtures, but I can't be convinced it should be a major component of woodland or water-side blends, as it sometimes is. An obvious solution is to contact a wildflower seed supplier and buy their grass mixture without any wildflowers (although not all will supply this); and then buy individual plant species separately and so produce your own mixture. Clearly, to do this meaningfully requires a working knowledge of the native plants that inhabit the environment you are trying to represent but the real difficulty is that without experience, it is hard to choose the optimum proportions. A useful compromise is to discover from the seed suppliers' catalogues the proportions used in the various ready-prepared mixtures and either add or leave out individual species to blend your own. One thing is worth stressing above all. You must use a grass mixture blended for the purpose. Lawn seed simply won't do; at least coarse lawn seed won't do as it is largely composed of vigorous hybrid rye grasses that are most unattractive and lank when in flower. A good grass blend offered by at least one seed company in the UK comprises the following and this is a good yardstick to use if you are blending your own:

Common bent (*Agrostis capillaris*): 10 per cent
Sweet vernal grass (*Anthoxanthum odoratum*):
  5 per cent
Quaking grass (*Briza media*): 5 per cent
Crested dogtail (*Cyanosurus cristatus*): 35 per cent
Red fescue (*Festuca rubra*): 25 per cent
Meadow barley (*Hordeum secalinum*): 5 per cent
Created hair-grass (*Koeleria macrantha*): 5 per cent
Small Timothy (*Phleum pratense*) 10 per cent

Sowing rates are about 4–5 grams per square metre of a grass and flower mixture or 1 gram per square metre for native flowers alone but as with any broadcast sowing, it's important to add a 'filler' to obtain uniform distribution. I use sawdust in a ratio by volume of about ten parts sawdust to one of seeds.

You can't grow every wildflower that takes your fancy so don't be too ambitious. At the last count, my native plant garden contained fifty-eight species and much as I would like others, I recognize it isn't practicable. I do try a few additions each season, generally species that are the food plants for insects I particularly want to attract. I always use strong well-grown plants to give them the best possible chance in competition with the existing vegetation and if they survive, all to the good. If not, I put it down to experience. And

over time, the proportions of the plants that make up your sowing will also change, just as happens naturally, as some species find the conditions in your garden more to their liking than others.

As your seeds germinate and seedlings emerge, so too will the residue of seeds derived from the natural population of perennial and annual weeds on the site. In my own plots, groundsel and shepherd's purse were particularly

*Quaking grass (*Briza media*) is one of several suitable species for a meadow grass mixture.*

prominent in the first winter. Don't be alarmed at this. They will tend to grow faster than your plants and soon stand out taller than the rest. As they do so, this is the moment to give the area its first gentle cut. A wheeled rotary lawnmower with the cutters set high will generally be satisfactory although some modern mowers have a powerful suction action than can uproot weak seedlings. I found it took relatively little time, and afforded more control, to go over the area initially with long-handled lawn shears to take the top off the weeds. Through the first autumn, winter and early spring, I also worked over the area several times with a long-handled daisy grubber and removed any emerging dandelions. By mid-spring in the second year, the perennials will be appearing increasingly strongly but annual weeds will still be there. This is the time for a further cut and it is here I want to introduce the biggest single aid to native plant gardening and a device of which I am enduringly appreciative – my long-handled powered hedge trimmer. This is of course invaluable for cutting high hedges but it is a remarkable tool with a two-stroke engine, a shaft around 64cm/25in long and, at the end, a normal reciprocating hedge trimmer blade but one that can be set at any

RIGHT, ABOVE: Some sedges naturally form large mounds and shouldn't be cut back to soil level in the same way as grasses. RIGHT, BELOW: In late summer, you will need to choose the most appropriate moment for 'hay-making'.

chosen angle. It was expensive but I can't now imagine native plant gardening without it.

There is little to do during the summer in your native plant garden except enjoy it. Any particularly vigorous plants should be removed and any large weeds that have survived or invaded should also be 'daisy-grubbed' or spot treated with glyphosate. I use the hedge trimmer once every week or two to keep the paths clear but little else is necessary. By early autumn, most of the seeds

will have set and the area should be fully cut. The long-handled hedge trimmer is then used for 'mowing' the meadow. Many books on native flower gardening suggest that wildflower meadows should be cut with a scythe. I can only conclude that the authors have never tried it or that they must live in some eighteenth-century rural Utopia where the sun always shines on the harvest, the meadow vegetation is never wet, the scythe has the blade of a razor and they themselves have the biceps of a country yokel. Believe me, it is unrealistic. But equally unrealistic is to cut the meadow, as is also often recommended, with a rotary mower – the suction will take away a large proportion of the precious seeds.

Think of cutting your meadow as haymaking in miniature. The plants should be cut down on a warm dry day to about 5cm/2in above soil and the residue allowed to lie for a week or so. During this time it should be turned with a fork or hay rake (the old farming operation of 'tedding'), not really to dry it but more importantly to ensure as many as possible of the seeds are shed.

When cutting your native plant meadow, be careful not to chop down any sedges (*Carex* species) or rushes (usually *Juncus* and *Luzula* species) you may have. They are typically although not exclusively plants for wet places and are most likely to be present in pond edge seed mixtures or to have been planted at the pond side individually. But they are much less adept than grasses and than herbaceous meadow perennial flowers at

regenerating from the base and by leaving them, you will also give the area some height and interest during the winter. The cyperus sedge (*Carex pseudocyperus*), for instance, is an easy-to-grow pond edge plant that looks attractive all year round – provided it is left to its own devices.

OTHER HABITATS

There will be small areas within your overall wildlife garden that aren't occupied by the general meadow plants and that can and should be used for special purposes. The most important is the pond edge. One of the biggest problems faced when creating an attractive pond in an informal setting (that is, one where you can't use slabs or other hard landscaping materials) lies in finding a way to conceal the edges of the liner in places where it drapes over the edges of the pond and on to the surrounding area. My preference is for cobbles tumbling into the water with a narrow area of turf on top. In the wildlife garden, the turf won't be mown and I advise leaving the edge completely uncut even in winter. It is important that the grasses aren't too vigorous and look appropriate so use the best quality turf containing the finest fescue grasses. As they develop, the grasses will tend to drape down towards the water and so soften the appearance of the cobbles. It is easy to plant into the turf with selected clumps of native plants (but do take care not to dig down too enthusiastically and cut through the liner itself). Outside the turf, try using use a pond edge seeding

mixture although if your experience with them is anything like mine, you will find the germination is fairly erratic and that planting with clumps of individual plants is a better long-term proposition.

Individual native marginal and water plants may be planted in the usual way in planting baskets although I use old weathered roofing tiles to conceal the baskets – they soon attract algal growth and blend attractively into the whole. It's also worth pouring sieved sub-soil mixed with the seed of small marginal species such as creeping Jenny (*Lysimachia nummularia*) over the cobbles. Even if only a few seeds germinate, the result is worth the effort as this speeds up slightly a process that will in any event occur naturally – soil and seeds will become lodged between the cobbles, plants will grow and very soon the whole will take on the semblance of a natural pond edge.

Choice of water plants must be made with care. Many are extremely vigorous although it is important to have some to provide cover for aquatic wild life and places for fish and amphibians to spawn. I use mainly water cress (*Rorippa nasturtium-aquaticum*), brooklime (*Veronica beccabunga*) and, more or less on the bank itself, water forget-me-not (*Myosotis scorpioides*), which serve the purpose admirably and are more manageable than most. Water mint

*Native water plants must be chosen with care. The yellow water lily (*Nuphar lutea*) is fine for lakes but not for most garden ponds.*

(*Mentha aquatica*) is another option with the appeal of a fragrant smell but it is vigorous. You will also perhaps want a water lily. There are only two native species and one of them, the yellow water lily, or brandy bottle (*Nuphar lutea*) has the largest leaves of any British plant (over 40cm/16in in diameter). Your pond will vanish beneath it in the first season. Grow instead the native white water lily (*Nymphaea alba*), still vigorous but more controllable. Like all my other water lilies, mine is in a terracotta pot 25cm/10in diameter.

The biggest difficulty facing the prospective native plant gardener with only limited space is presented by trees. How do you grow native trees, with their attendant importance for attracting wildlife, without casting the entire area into complete shade? Planting small trees and then cutting them down once they reach about 6m/20ft in height is one option, although you may find your goose well and truly cooked if you live in a statutory Conservation Area where every tree by that stage will automatically have acquired legal protection. I have in a sense circumvented the problem by what seems to me the quintessence of commonsense gardening – growing fastigiate variants of native trees. Narrowly upright, these take up little room, cast little shade and yet are nonetheless valuable in breaking a skyline and screening buildings or structures beyond. And most importantly, they will attract at least some of the wildlife that is dependent on them. Not all native trees occur in fastigiate form although some, like the oaks, exist in several. Among those I have are mountain ash (*Sorbus aucuparia* 'Fastigiata'), hawthorn (*Crataegus monogyna* 'Stricta'), beech (*Fagus sylvatica* 'Dawyck'), broad-leaved lime (*Tilia platyphyllos* 'Fastigiata'), yew (*Taxus baccata* 'Fastigiata'), elder (*Sambucus nigra* 'Pyramidalis'), hornbeam (*Carpinus betulus* 'Frans Fontaine') and two pedunculate oaks (*Quercus robur* f. *fastigiata* and *Q. r.* 'Hungaria').

Planting of native woodland herbaceous species is only worthwhile if you already have fairly mature trees in the garden. And it isn't easy even then because the area will almost certainly be dry and your woodland seed mixture won't germinate unless you keep it constantly irrigated. I have achieved the best success with individual plantings rather than sowing, using strongly growing species like dog's mercury (*Mercurialis perennis*), figwort (*Scrophularia nodosa*) and wild strawberry (*Fragaria vesca*) – an excellent and vigorous ground-cover species even in really dry places. Stinging nettle (*Urtica dioica*), an essential plant in any wildlife garden because of its importance as a food plant for some of the most beautiful butterflies (including red admiral, peacock, comma, small tortoiseshell and painted lady), will also grow fairly well under trees in light shade and this conveniently tucks it out of the way. One exception to the general lack of success with seed comes with that invaluable and lovely biennial the foxglove (*Digitalis purpurea*) which may take two years initially to

germinate but which then soon builds up a self-sustaining population.

I have created an interesting and valuable additional habitat with a small pile of loosely mounded rocks and an old gate post that I have used to resemble a tumbledown dry-stone wall in miniature. I laid permeable membrane over the soil first to minimize the growth of existing meadow perennials and have found that provided there is at least some soil among the rocks, plants such as herb Robert (*Geranium robertianum*), navelwort (*Umbilicaria rupestris*), wallflower (*Erysimum cheiri*), several species of fern including common polypody (*Polypodium vulgare*), and one of my favourite wildflowers, yellow toadflax (*Linaria vulgaris*), establish with little difficulty. Slightly harder to germinate and establish but most rewarding when it does is ivy-leaved toadflax (*Cymbalaria muralis*). You will find that a large population of invertebrates, especially spiders, will soon build up too and, if you live in an appropriate part of the country, you may be lucky and attract lizards. You will almost invariably also attract snails, but these present relatively little problem in the wildlife garden and I know that our thrush population has increased in consequence.

A particularly popular group of wildflowers are the cornfield annuals, species that have achieved their greatest fame and notoriety as weeds among cereal crops but which are nonetheless extremely attractive. Those offered most commonly are corn chamomile (*Anthemis arvensis*), field poppy

(*Papaver rhoeas*), cornflower (*Centaurea cyanus*), corn marigold (*Chrysanthemum segetum*) and corn cockle (*Agrostemma githago*). Modern farming and modern herbicides all but finished off some of them in the 1960s, although organic farming methods and set-aside have since allowed some to re-establish and become familiar once more. Farming friends of an older generation still wince when they see field poppy in flower – even if it is in my garden. All species will give a modest display in the first season if sown among perennials but disappear through being competed out thereafter and it is much better to set apart an area specifically for them. As annuals, they of course need different management from the perennials and they should perpetuate themselves perfectly well by self-sowing each year. If yours don't, you may wish to re-sow them every autumn, after the crop debris has been cleared away, but at half the normal rate (around two grams per square metre) to augment what has been shed naturally. For reasons that I don't fully understand, but which must be related to varying seed maturity and dormancy, the proportion of the different species that emerges seems to vary each year. Among them, I have also sown scarlet pimpernel (*Anagallis arvensis* subsp. *arvensis*) and common field-speedwell (*Veronica persica*), which flower and seed before the tall species mature. Be aware, however, that cornfield weeds are all fairly tall plants and in an exposed situation will readily be blown over. (In cereal fields, they occur as scattered individuals and derive support from the stiff cereal stems.) I have an area of cornfield annuals at one side of the native plant garden, in effect to represent the edge of a field, and have placed a lightweight rustic fence alongside it to enhance the appearance and to give some physical support – in strong winds or driving rain, the plants are blown against the fence rather than being flattened across the adjacent stepping-stone path.

With our additional land, we acquired a large old stone trough that had originally been on one of the village farms and this gave me the opportunity for some rather unusual additions. Conventional wisdom says that stone troughs are ideal for growing alpines. And so they are, but I wanted the trough in the native plant garden. So, much to everyone's surprise, I have devoted two thirds of it to native alpines. The commonest reaction has been 'I didn't know there were any'. I suppose it depends on how you define alpine. Suffice it to say that I have amassed an interesting little collection of native plants from British, mainly Scottish mountains. The trough is tipped slightly for drainage and the acid-loving species in their acidic compost are 'upstream', the alkaline loving

PAGE 140: Buddleia davidii *will attract butterflies to your garden but won't provide food for their larvae. PAGE 141: I keep a separate area for cornfield plants such as cornflower (*Centaurea cyanus*) and corncockle (*Agrostemma githago*).*

species at the drainage hole end. This is to avoid having alkaline water draining through the acidic compost because acid-loving plants are highly intolerant of calcium in the soil. The reverse isn't true – mildly acidic water draining through alkaline soil is of no consequence.

The one third of the trough that isn't occupied by native alpines is occupied by native insectivorous plants. In common with many botanists, I find insectivorous plants both fascinating and beautiful but it is isn't always appreciated that there are several British species – three native sundews (*Drosera*), two or three native butterworts (*Pinguicula*) and odd naturalized pockets of the pitcher plant (*Sarracenia purpurea*), introduced from North America. All insectivorous plants live naturally in boggy places, devoid of nutrients, which explains why they have adapted to using insects as an alternative food source. It's essential therefore to grow them in a low-nutrient acidic medium, such as peat and Sphagnum moss, and to maintain a regular supply of water. I have simply taken a micro-bore pipe from a rainwater butt containing a small pump (insectivorous plants must be watered with rainwater) to provide programmed irrigation to the trough. It works most effectively.

In addition to the native plants, your garden should include other features to attract wildlife. The most obvious are bird boxes and bird feeders and, if you buy from one of the specialist suppliers, you will not only be able to choose a durable box carefully designed for the particular birds you want to attract but also advice on exactly where best to position it. In general, bird boxes are ideally positioned facing south or south-west and, although they needn't be very high off the ground (many birds after all nest in hedges), most are generally more successful if partly concealed among trees and shrubs. Exception are the mortar or resin boxes designed for swallows and martins, which should be attached just below the eaves of a building. Choose several types of bird feeder including bird tables, wire tubes for peanuts and clear plastic tubes for sunflower and other seeds. If your garden is anything like mine, I strongly advise you to buy squirrel-proof bird feeders, the feeding tube of which is enclosed in a wire cage. Like most naturalists, I am in two minds about grey squirrels and took a particularly dim view when we installed an owl box about 6m/20ft high in an atlas cedar in the main garden only to find that a squirrel had decided it provided ideal summer quarters. I await with some interest the events that take place when in due course, a tawny owl does move in.

Almost as popular as bird boxes now are bat boxes, which are intended to provide summer roosts for garden-visiting bats. (Bats look for other, quite different sites, generally underground, for their winter hibernation.) Siting is even more critical here however and it is essential to follow the advice of the manufacturers or specialist bat conservation societies. I have a bat box on the

the artificial mason bee nest was generously occupied in its first season. Red mason bees (*Osmia rufa*), an excellent pollinating species, were almost forming a queue to lay their eggs inside and add a parcel of nectar for their future offspring before sealing the tube ends with mud.

It is also important to provide places where mosses, fungi and lichens can grow and beneath which small terrestrial invertebrates can hide. A pile of logs is a *sine qua non* for a wildlife garden but, once in place, they must be left undisturbed. You need have no concern that, like tree stumps, they might attract honey fungus. There is still far too widespread a belief that any toadstool in a garden is honey fungus and likely to cause harm. Neither is remotely true and I suggest you obtain 60cm/24in lengths of various hardwoods, including oak, beech, ash and birch from a local tree surgeon in order to encourage as wide a range of species as possible.

I admit, quite unashamedly, that my wildlife garden is nature sanitized. The sanitation is what makes the difference between a wildlife garden and a wilderness and to do anything else is pointless unless you own rolling acres of real countryside. In limited space you must remember to keep a close eye on dandelions, sow-thistles, bindweed and other aggressive and invasive species, and to remove them routinely, or your 'wildlife garden' will be neither use nor ornament, neither a thing of beauty nor a haven for choice animal species.

gable end of an outbuilding and have plans in due course to adapt the interior of the roof of this or another building for bat roosting. One important factor in the siting of bat boxes is the need for flying space in the approach to the box.

Boxes and hides are now obtainable for attracting and providing shelter for bees, lacewings, ladybirds and other creatures and if you are fortunate, these may add to the populations that will inevitably be attracted to your garden by the plant life. I was delighted when the tiny cylinder of cardboard tubes that comprises

Bird boxes are essential in a wildlife garden, but choose the most appropriate box for each species and position them with care.

GARDEN DESIGN

GARDEN DESIGN

I have been quoted as having said that garden design is the great con trick of modern horticulture. What I in fact said was the notion that anyone can design their own garden is the great con trick of modern popular horticulture: not quite the same thing. But I would say that, you might suppose, earning part of my living by designing gardens for other people. The reality is that there aren't enough professional designers to go round – even if everyone wanted and could afford to engage professional help (they don't, thank goodness). Countless thousands of gardeners want to create and build their own gardens, and will gain enormous pleasure and satisfaction from it, just as I did. My real point is that you can't expect to achieve the same results as quickly, you can't necessarily expect to appreciate all the options and certainly you won't see all the pitfalls of your site without the experience of having seen many other sites and many other gardens. To suggest otherwise is the con trick.

Every site is different, every gardener's needs and likes are different and some projects present much greater challenges than others. What I hope to do in this chapter is to give some pointers, ideas and suggestions to guide you in the most appropriate directions, pose questions that you should consider and provide possible

---

A delightful combination of plants and structural features making the most of a narrow town garden.

answers, with the objective of helping you achieve your goals as straightforwardly and effectively as possible.

I have never thought that garden design, on an amateur or professional level, can be done to best advantage without an understanding of as many as possible of the options that are available – and why they are available. Garden design is, after all, an art form; it is four-dimensional art, in contrast to the three dimensions of sculpture and the two dimensions of painting, and few sculptors or painters would begin work without having looked at a fair range of other artists' work. In garden design, time, the fourth dimension, is the special bit. Unlike sculptures and paintings, gardens start to change as soon as you have created them and go on changing year by year. It is the visionary ability to see ahead and to understand the changes that makes the difference between a great and successful garden designer and any other type of artist. It is often said that the famous landscape garden designers, such as Brown, Kent and Repton, displayed this far-sighted talent to perfection. They were planting trees (generally fairly small trees) and had to think ahead a century or more to envisage the finished effect. It was a striking ability but then trees are big, the total number of individual plants, even in a big landscaped garden is relatively small and most people know what a mature specimen looks like. I'm not at all sure that being able to project ahead two seasons and visualize your herbaceous

border after you have planted it isn't almost as perceptive – although I grant that anything you need to change and correct is immeasurably simpler to do.

GARDEN HISTORY

In creating your own garden, you will, incidentally or, I hope, deliberately, see other gardens, great gardens, most good, some not so good, that other people have created over the years. Doing this helps to understand what lies behind them so you can appreciate what lessons you can learn yourself. You can't of course see every garden, not even every garden in your own area. But that doesn't matter. I do urge you to see as wide a range of styles as possible; it doesn't even matter if you don't like the majority. That is all part of the learning process. And equally important is to have a basic grasp of how gardens today came to be as they are, what has happened in the past.

It hardly needs to be said that the way we live now is very different from the way our gardening ancestors lived, but the modern garden is nonetheless the embodiment of all that has gone before. Rather than see today's garden as an isolated entity, frozen in time, I think it's both instructive and interesting to realize how our present-day gardens evolved. This should help you to understand and appreciate the range of styles you will see on your travels. Before outlining my basic list of modern garden styles therefore, I want to offer a thumbnail sketch of British gardening history.

Until little more than a century ago, the specifically ornamental garden in Britain was the grand garden. Poor and ordinary folk were too busy with survival to have time or room for such things and the bulk of their gardening activity was centred on the home vegetable plot, something that really survives in Britain today only as the crofter's cabbage garden or the allotment. Nonetheless, by allowing some of the more attractive weeds to survive, they became the unwitting catalysts for the development of a gardening style that is quintessentially British, one that has remained unchanged for hundred of years – the hotchpotch of flowers, vegetables, fruit and animals that became known as the cottage garden. And ironically, this is many people's ideal garden today, a Utopia for urban estate and village home alike.

The earliest ornamental gardens of any significance in Britain were those built by the Romans and the Romano-British. None survives but it does appear that their planting styles reflected the gardens of Rome itself. The plants they used were a blend of the herbal and ornamental, usually planted in lines or squares but often in containers too – the Romans did wonderful things with terracotta. Roman gardens were highly advanced but, after their departure from Britain in the fifth century AD, there are few records of any gardening activity here until it surfaced again five hundred years later in the kitchen and herbal gardens of the monasteries. None of these gardens survives either, although we have documentary accounts of their appearance and a few fine replicas have been built. The typical medieval monastery garden, like the Roman gardens before them, had arbours, courtyards, raised beds and quadrangles. They were places to harvest food but also for contemplation. Then, over the next two hundred years, the ornamental garden became an adjunct to the stately home and the palace. Intricate geometric patterns of plants were produced by training and pruning; labour was almost limitless.

By the middle of the sixteenth century, the Tudor garden had its mazes and mounts. The seventeenth century saw more trees and shrubs in the Jacobean garden, followed in turn by influences from the Continent – from France and Holland, and later, following the popularity of the Grand Tour, from Italy. Although they made a considerable impact at the time, none has had important and enduring influences on the modern home garden. The garden was formal and it remained so until early in the eighteenth century when Lancelot 'Capability' Brown (1716–83) and later Humphry Repton (1752–1818) led the abandonment of huge, formal, rigid geometric patterns, confined the flower garden close to the house and created instead sweeping landscapes. They were shapers of the countryside rather than gardeners

and so inevitably their immediate influence on small home gardens was minimal. I like to believe, however, that it was their notion of a remodelled, more natural environment, combined improbably with the total informality of the cottage garden, that was to surface in the embryonic modern home garden of the nineteenth century.

As the British Empire expanded throughout the Victorian period, (at its peak in 1901 it spanned a quarter of the land surface of the world), vast numbers of new plants were collected and introduced to British gardens. Many wealthy landowners took up plant collecting and had impressive gardens with a large staff to match. Their new acquisitions were grown either in beds or in borders. William Cobbett, in his book

The Tudor House garden in Southampton is a rare example of an accurate replica Tudor planting scheme.

The English Gardener published just before the start of the Victorian age, in 1828, described the difference: a bed contained predominantly one type of flower, a border was a mixture. Cobbett would have been familiar with hardy annuals, biennials and bulbs such as tulips but it wasn't until around 1840 that a fall in the price of glass led to the much wider availability of greenhouses and cold frames. It was this that encouraged an interest in half-hardy annuals, plants like pelargoniums, tagetes, petunias, fuchsias, verbena,

salvia, ageratum and lobelia, so familiar to our bedding and container schemes today. They filled formal beds up and down the land.

But mid-Victorian gardeners gradually came to rebel against this formal bedding style. Inspired by what Brown and Repton had done for the landscape, they began to bring elements of informality and the cottage garden to the fore. One of the aims was something we recognize as so important today: to produce a mixed flower border that had colour for months rather than just a few weeks without the need for replanting. So the border that came to such pre-eminence in the later years of Victoria's reign was the herbaceous border, largely of perennials. The Irishman William Robinson (1838–1935) synthesized many of the guiding principles in his book *The English Flower Garden*, published in 1883. Gertrude Jekyll (1843–1932) took Robinson's ideas to heart and adapted them to create herbaceous borders for the houses and gardens designed by her friend Edwin Lutyens.

The first half of the twentieth century saw times of war and economic depression and meant the returning of the home garden to its role of providing food. The 'Dig for Victory' campaign that encouraged the growing of fresh vegetables to supplement the nation's diet has been well-

Many of our now familiar bedding plants became popular with the increase in the use of glasshouses in the early nineteenth century.

documented. After the end of the Second World War, people wanted a change from the drab and merely useful and longed again for colourful flowers in their gardens; roses were popular and bedding plants in patriotic red, white and blue. A generation or two later, such gaudy colours were out of fashion and pastel became *de rigeur*. But, more importantly, the whole approach to gardening came to be challenged. A generation grew up that questioned the use of artificial (or indeed, and less advisedly, any) added chemicals, either on farm or on garden, that wanted 'pure and wholesome' food and that wanted to do its bit in saving the planet; it was a movement that led to what I call 'free-range gardening'.

The typical garden in Britain today is smaller than 200m²/240 square yards in area. As gardens

Herbaceous borders appear in many forms – this is a double version – but all require considerable maintenance.

have become smaller, (or we want to use them for more activities so they simply seem smaller), the plants we grow must really earn their place. In a large stately home garden for instance, setting aside a large area for a double herbaceous border through which to walk in summer was quite feasible. Out of season one would simply move to another area of the garden (or another house). In small modern gardens, by contrast, there might be room for one small border, visible all year round from the house. It makes far more sense for the border to contain a mixture of plants, one that offers something in each season: bulbs in spring, herbaceous perennials and annuals in summer, berries, foliage and the bark of shrubs in autumn, evergreen colours and shapes in winter.

Many people wish to spend less time on gardening chores, staking, weeding and digging and more on planning colour schemes and using their garden for leisure. The garden industry is very aware of this and now offers us a variety of labour-saving tools and labour-saving plants – dwarf varieties that need no staking, weed suppressing ground-cover shrubs that need no pruning, and dwarf rye grass mixtures for lawns that are harder wearing and need less mowing. The deep-bed system for growing vegetables has reduced the amount of digging needed while mulching beds and borders has lessened the need for weeding and watering. Growing plants in containers close to the house fits in well with many people's way of life. Half-hardy plants no longer have to be raised but can be bought at almost any stage of growth.

An increasing environmental awareness has led to an interest in organic gardening and native plant gardening. Even perennials have been rescued from the border and experiments are now under way to grow them in more natural groupings with the aim of reducing maintenance. Vegetable growing, sadly, has declined from its 'Dig for Victory' peak, although garden ownership is higher than it has ever been and more recently allotment gardening has seen something of a return. The motives for home-grown produce today are rather different. They have less to do with self-sufficiency than with a wish to eat wholesome food, grown without artificial chemical supplements and yet without the surcharge that attaches to goods from the 'organic' counter at the local supermarket.

Now more than ever before, gardeners are influenced by fashion and marketing. Part of this is of course is due to greater communication through the broadcasting and publishing media, but the growth of garden centres, out of town superstores and garden shows has also played an essential part. Even non-gardeners are encouraged to think of their 'room outdoors' and there are plenty of people willing to help them fill it, if not with plants then with furniture, barbecues, swimming pools, summer houses and the other 'necessities' of modern gardening life.

GARDEN STYLES

Although I constantly find myself saying that every garden is different and I don't really like to categorize, I do draw clients' attention to the fact that the garden styles most popular today only really number about seven or eight. Trying to decide in advance on a garden style rather than buying things on impulse will help ensure that your house, the plants and the non-living parts of the garden all work together to create a pleasurable environment.

In a small garden, you may be restricted to a single design style but larger gardens are often most successfully subdivided into smaller areas or, as they are sometimes called today, garden rooms. This is certainly nothing new in garden design – some of the oldest gardens of which we have any knowledge were subdivided in a fairly regimented way into quite separate areas. But it is also a feature of much of the best of twentieth century garden design and one of the earlier modern examples of the genre in England is that pivotally important garden: Hidcote in Gloucestershire. There, a windswept Cotswold hilltop was divided up by hedges, partly to provide wind protection but also to enclose quite distinct formal and informal areas, typical of the increasing tendency today not simply to subdivide but for each area to embody a rather different approach.

Formal, classical, cottage, even Oriental may all be included within the same site. I have done

just this in my own garden and created an eclectic blend incorporating elements that range from a replica seventeenth-century knot to a wildlife garden. If this style appeals to you, do keep the number of separate components appropriate to the overall size of your site or you will end up with less of a garden and more of a jigsaw; and do ensure the parts really are discrete and well separated off from each other or the impact of each will be lost.

What follows is a brief discussion of just some of the possible approaches that you might want to consider. Remember that not all of them are mutually exclusive.

The European Formal Garden

Here, the hard landscaping is usually based on a geometric shape, often symmetrical. At least some of the plants are used in regular patterns; clipped yew or box are popular choices but formally trained roses, lavender and other flowering shrubs play a part. Lawns, if used, are neat, regular and well-maintained but paving or stone chips are often more appropriate, especially in smaller areas. Attractive containers and

This part of my garden has been described as 'essentially English', although in reality the 'English' garden style is totally eclectic.

ornaments made of sympathetic materials play an important part. Today, the formal approach probably finds its greatest value in small town gardens but it is a style I recommend widely because it is low-maintenance, has year-round appeal and I find immensely satisfying. My own formal knot garden generally attracts the most comment and admiration of all the areas of my own garden. The initial costs can be fairly high simply because yew and box, two of the most important ingredients, are rather expensive and if you skimp on quantity, you will have to wait years before your line of little plants begins to look like formal hedging.

The English Informal Garden

There is an absence here of very obvious patterns and order. The arrangement seems more natural, with the plants in irregular drifts rather than straight rows. Paths and lawns should flow and wander and there are relatively few straight lines. Structures of wood and natural or replica stone are often used and the rigid shape of boundaries is concealed with plants. It is this style of gardening that has spawned what many people consider the crowning glory of English gardening,

LEFT: *The English informal garden – wonderful in high summer but certainly not a low-maintenance option. PAGES 156-7: The classical garden, superb when done well but seldom attempted, although it is appropriate for both large and small areas.*

the herbaceous border, although in the modern home garden, its place has largely been taken by the mixed border in which a framework of shrubs provides a skeletal structure – and gives you something to look at in winter (see page 83). The informal garden isn't a low-price, low-maintenance option, particularly for a big area. Initial costs are fairly high because of the large number of plants required and if you want less common types, you may have to search widely and pay proportionately. Maintenance is high because of the regular attention necessary to stake, tie in, prune, feed and possibly water too.

The Classical Garden

Like the European formal garden, this style takes a highly disciplined approach with formally clipped green hedges, a symmetrical layout and classically inspired ornaments or, if space allows, buildings – pergolas, arches or courtyards. It takes its inspiration, however, not from the recent centuries of European history but from Classical times. The garden is uncluttered and relaxing but impractical for people who collect plants for their own sake and not really appropriate for those with young children. The Classical garden is rarely successful in a small space and although reproduction 'Roman' and 'Greek' statuary is now available at every garden centre (there must be a Venus de Milo factory somewhere) it is the garden style that most often fails today. I say this for several reasons: partly because it really needs bright light

and baking heat to look its best; partly because one of the characteristic plants, the pencil-shaped Mediterranean cypress (*Cupressus sempervirens*), isn't hardy enough for most parts of Britain (although the similarly shaped North American *Calocedrus decurrens* is a good substitute); but mainly because people can't resist using modern plants (and, worst of all, modern flowers) to decorate it and the whole ends up looking frankly naff. But when it is created with discipline and does work, it is wonderful.

The Cottage Garden

It's a modern lifestyle paradox that books and magazines about the countryside and country

BELOW: The cottage garden in its modern form is a 'do what you like' mixture of informal plantings. BELOW, RIGHT: The gravelled area with Mediterranean plants is an elegant style, popularized by Beth Chatto at her garden in Essex.

living tend to be bought by people who live in towns and hanker (in theory at least) for the wide world beyond. So the cottage garden is possibly the type of garden that most people, town and city dwellers above all, would place at the top of their wish list. Yet the original cottage garden was nothing like the popular impression gained from countless chocolate boxes or seen through the artistic filter of a Helen Allingham watercolour. The real cottage garden was the garden of the rural poor, a rather miserable and untidy place for much of the year where people, chickens and pigs lived in close juxtaposition and interdependence. The modern cottage garden is a highly sanitized version, without the pigs and generally the chickens too. Flowers, herbs and vegetables grow together in informal plantings. At least some of the flowering interest is produced by plants self-seeding but although the planting is highly informal, careful management is required to keep it under control and to

distinguish between the good and the bad among wild species; a cottage garden still needs weeding. Ornaments and structures are simple – hazel hurdles, picket fencing, relatively plain terracotta pots and rustic arches. Yes, this may be one of the most popular of all gardening styles, yet it is arguably the most difficult; and it is highly labour intensive.

The Architectural Garden

An inappropriate name I always think because the architectural garden generally uses little architecture in the conventional sense but does employ striking and generally exotic plants to create points of attention. There is bold and very obvious planting with specimens chosen for their shape rather than flower colour. Grasses, bamboos and large foliage plants are often used in very conspicuous groupings with modern hard landscaping materials. This is a low-maintenance garden but one for people whose interests lie more in art than in horticulture.

The Oriental Garden

Ever since the countries of the Far East, especially China and Japan, became seriously accessible to visitors from the West in the mid-nineteenth century, their way of life has fascinated and intrigued. This is especially true of their gardens, which are visually so very different from those in the West. Today, replica stone lanterns, pots and other containers embellished with Oriental script and other typical features are on sale everywhere. The range of stone chips, pebbles and cobbles is ever growing and many of the ingredients are there for a garden embodying much of the Oriental style to be created anywhere in the world.

An Oriental style garden (at least a fairly large one) is the only garden in which I would have significant areas of wood – the decking much beloved of modern instant gardening. But that's a personal axe I grind – I just don't like it and by and large find it impractical. The characteristic plants of Oriental gardens, such as pines, camellias, peonies and ferns, are readily obtainable. Even bamboos, which used to present something of a problem because of the relative tenderness and invasiveness of many, are now available in ever-increasing variety with a good selection of non-invasive and hardy species and varieties.

There is no need to understand the underlying Buddhist teachings or to be an adherent to the principles of Feng Shui to be able to create in your own garden an extremely appealing area with a Oriental appearance and feel. If you want to delve more deeply into the ideology of Oriental horticulture you will no doubt be richly rewarded. But if you don't, you shouldn't be put off by criticisms that you are not being purist. My tiny Orient-inspired garden area has been developed for no better reason than that I like it; and it is a memorial to a friend who loved Japan. I have

visited the countries of the Far East and seen 'the real thing' but I don't feel any guilt at having created a little pastiche; nor should you. It will be of relatively low cost and low-maintenance. And if done carefully, it should offer one of the essential features of Oriental gardening in being a place that is both restful and relaxing: a small area for contemplation.

The Wildlife Garden

I have discussed wildlife gardening in some detail in Chapter Six and won't therefore describe it in detail here, other than to say that because of the large numbers of seeding native plants, it makes especial sense to separate a wildlife area by hedges if you don't want too much intrusion into the rest of the garden.

The Idiosyncratic Garden

I use the term idiosyncratic for want of something better to describe gardens that are uniquely peculiar to their owners, that display some highly unusual or unexpected features. Among many examples I have seen are: a garden furnished with mirrors in every border so the viewer sees himself among the plants, a garden where the soil was covered with black tarmac and small groups of orange flowers placed in planting holes, a garden where trees were replaced with aluminium poles and one I designed called 'A garden in four movements' where a water course flowed through a quartered garden at varying speeds and with varying degrees of serenity, reflecting the four time signatures of a symphony. As long as it doesn't frighten horses and old ladies (or, more seriously, upset the neighbours), you can do as you like. But don't be surprised if the unorthodox throws up horticultural or environmental problems you don't anticipate. Whenever I see the increasingly common gardens at the Chelsea Flower Show (where they win Gold Medals) that incorporate large areas of shining white stone or concrete, spectacular panels of polished stainless steel or

PAGES 160–61: The Oriental garden is almost the only style in which I can appreciate decking – and, as in this small private garden, is not difficult to create. LEFT: Perhaps the most extreme example of an idiosyncratic garden is this one I found in Holland some years ago.

pastel-painted buildings, I inevtiably find myself saying 'bird droppings' (or words to that effect).

The 'Instant' Garden

There will be an expectation that I should say something about that *sine qua non* of television makeover programmes, decking; and about the programmes themselves. My interest and passion is in showing people how to garden in the hope they will derive as much pleasure from it as I do. It doesn't matter if they want to devote half an hour or ten hours a week to the hobby; provided they do it and enjoy it, I will be delighted. But I'm not interested in the notion that a garden can be created in a weekend, that a meaningful garden can be created without the owner knowing anything about it or having any say in it, or that the creation of an 'instant garden' is the end of the story.

As I have said already, gardens are four-dimensional, and so as soon as the film crew has departed on Sunday evening, the 'garden' they have left behind begins to change and the owners need to be aware of this and prepared for it. If people want to use gardens as a medium for entertainment, good luck to them; it has nothing to do with gardening as I understand it. And decking? Fine in small doses for Oriental gardens, especially where it is to be looked at rather than walked on. In other gardens or larger areas, a waste of wonderful planting space, unsightly within a few years, and very often hideously slippery when it rains.

DESIGN FOR LIVING

Before I will even begin to consider a garden design, I tell clients that a full measured ground survey will be required. I don't perform this myself but engage professional surveyors and if you have a fairly large or intricate existing garden or plot, it's a course I would recommend to you. There are many frustrations inherit in designing gardens and you can do without the added burden of trying to position features by guesswork, only to discover when the work is underway and materials purchased, that things wont fit exactly as you expected. If you don't want this expense, then do the best you can yourself with a long tape measure and make a scale plan. I can't emphasize too strongly that you can only create a design, whether of an entire garden or a single plot or feature, if you have a scale plan of what is there already. Make a point of including careful estimates of the spread of existing trees – the span of the branches will indicate where shade is likely to be greatest while roughly the same span below ground will be the spread of the roots and indicate the area where plants are likely to face serious dryness and competition.

Make a careful note too of something that many people overlook – the compass directions. The difference between a garden facing north and one facing south can be critical to the success of particular designs or plants. Note down too the positions of nearby buildings or large features in neighbouring gardens which cast shadows at certain times of the day. And take plenty of photographs. Film (or, better still, a digital disc) is cheap and there's nothing like a snapshot to jog the memory when, in the leafless middle of winter, you are trying to recall just how something even as familiar as your own garden looks in the summer.

Climate, location and geology (as it's manifest through the types of underlying rock and soil) all play their part in determining how well plants will succeed in a given situation, but when designing and planning how a garden will appear and function, the needs of the people using it are at least as important. And these in turn depend on their lifestyle and, very often, their age. During our lives, there will be periods when we have time for gardening but relatively little money to spend on it; later, we may have more money available but are frustrated by lack of time to put changes into effect. Later still, it may not be time or money but physical strength that is in short supply. So, when planning your garden, try to ensure it matches your current needs, and ideally, that it can be adapted as those needs change. In this way, you'll gain maximum enjoyment from it and minimize, although not of course remove, the frustrations. The planning and design of a garden is particularly important if you or members of your family have special needs because factors such as safety and access will take precedence over aesthetic considerations and later in the chapter I have some remarks about gardening for the disabled and gardening with children.

The topography of the site – the humps, hollows and slopes – can influence the ease with which digging or lawn mowing can be performed, but should be considered positively too. A slope is always the best position for a rock garden; the top of a slope is the best place in an overall sloping garden for a fairly formal pool while the foot of a slope is best for an informal one where natural spilling over of water at the edges enables the margins to be softened with bog and waterside plants. The base of a hollow or even the foot of a slope is often a poor place for a fruit garden because dense, cold, frosty air accumulates there and will damage the blossom and such a site is also no place for slightly tender or early blossoming ornamentals. Conversely, the top of a slope is often a windy place and this too will make for an unproductive fruit garden because pollinating insects are blown away. Does your garden have special and unusual natural features?

Today's garden must satisfy the needs of the garden owners and their families, as well as being relatively easy and inexpensive to maintain.

Among those that are valuable and important enough to justify reorganizing other garden activities are a natural outcrop of rock, offering you the chance to have a real rock garden, and a stream or even a wet ditch, around which you can plant a bog garden.

The only already existing plants worth considering seriously in a garden design are trees because they are the only types of vegetation that can't be moved or quickly replaced. Many very good gardens are largely designed around one or a few mature trees as these generally dictate where much of the light and shade lies and, because they draw heavily on the food and water reserves of the soil, also dictate where you can't place vegetable and fruit gardens or mixed borders. The presence of trees, especially deciduous trees will also influence the positioning of the pools and the greenhouse; neither of which benefit from shade or falling leaves. If, as part of your design or re-design, you feel that one or more existing trees should be removed, do remember that unlike every other plant in your garden, trees present special problems. First, because of their size and weight, their removal could well be a task for a professional, but even more importantly, because they may have legal protection (see page 28).

Be sure to position features thoughtfully. A vegetable and herb garden must have as much sun as possible and should be both functional and attractive, both ends being served by having it as close as possible to the kitchen. When positioning purely ornamental beds and borders, be sure to place them where they can be appreciated at the time of year they will be at their best. This is most important in relation to plants grown for winter colour; there's little point in putting them at the furthest point from the house where no one will venture in winter. And do ensure the garden is designed for labour-saving maintenance. I've mentioned how the choice of plants and use of particular techniques can be important but the basic design of the garden is significant too. Good examples of annoying and time-consuming gardening tasks are trying to mow twists and corners of a lawn that are too small for the mower and are therefore either left untidy or must be cut laboriously with shears, and having a gravel path where something solid would be better. One adjoining a lawn is visually lovely although you must be prepared for occasionally having to brush stones from the grass but a gravel path adjoining a vegetable plot can be a nightmare as you walk from soil to gravel and pick up quantities of the path on your muddy footwear.

Creating a false illusion of space is not difficult in most gardens, and very rewarding too. Give the impression that there are a great many plants in your garden whilst at the same time filling relatively little of the area with them. The simplest way to achieve this apparent conjuring trick is to keep the centre of the garden open (with a lawn is the easiest way) and confine most of your

more detailed planning of plant colour and shape. Individuals' ideas of which colour combinations give the greatest pleasure vary enormously. And as with other areas of life, colour fashions come and go in gardening although changes tend to be rather slower to put into effect. I have no wish to try and tell anyone which colours or colour combinations they should use in their gardens. I do want however to indicate a few, fairly generally accepted principles of colour perception and appreciation. Most people wouldn't argue, for example, that among individual colours, reds and oranges are perceived as being hot and aggressive while blues, greens and whites are cool and restful.

For colour combinations, a colour wheel can be used to demonstrate different effects. Here the spectral colours of white light (red, orange, yellow, green, blue, indigo and violet) are drawn as segments of a wheel. Adjacent colours are then seen to harmonize; colours on the opposite side of the wheel make strong contrasts. These strong contrasts don't appeal to everyone and are often referred to as 'colour clashes' but there are occasions when they can be very effective. The combination of certain yellows with certain blues, for instance, is one that I find very pleasing in part of my own garden.

When 'painting' your garden, bear in mind that unlike real paints, more plant colours are available at certain times of the year than others. Early spring, for instance, is predominately a

plants to the periphery. This also has the advantage of obscuring the boundary fence or wall, so making it impossible to see where your property ends. This effect can be improved still further if there is open space beyond your garden (fields or parkland for instance) that can be glimpsed through gaps in these marginal plantings. And make good use of curves in lawns, beds, borders and paths to suggest that there is something beyond what can actually be seen. Placing a focal point so that it is glimpsed through an archway or a gap between two plantings also helps to take the eye a long way and enhance the feeling of distance. It really does all boil down eventually to common sense.

Having developed your ideas on the overall structure of your garden, you will want to begin

---

Colour in the garden, as in the home, is a highly personal matter. What is a delight to one person can be an eyesore to another.

season of yellows and oranges, the height of summer brings the greatest variety while autumn brings browns, oranges and reds but rather few blues. It will always be easier to follow nature's inclinations rather than fight them; but by all means create a few surprises seeking out unusually coloured plants by hunting through nursery catalogues.

Colour can be used in your garden in two main ways: group together plants of predominately one colour or blend them. At its extreme, the single colour approach is often seen in white gardens (not surprisingly as there is only one shade of white) or silver borders. In a mixed or herbaceous border, I can do no better than refer you to Gertrude Jekyll. In the early part of this century, she experimented for many years with long deep borders in her own garden at Munstead Wood in Surrey. She used intense, strong colours like oranges and reds in the centre and gradually introduced paler colour at the ends.

DESIGNING FOR THE ELDERLY OR DISABLED
Not so long ago, this topic was scarcely given any thought. Things have changed partly because many people who have gardened all of their lives now wish to continue doing so, with relative ease, as they become old and infirm. Perhaps even

The raised bed is a wonderful device for less able gardeners or those confined to wheelchairs.

more importantly, gardening itself is now seen as a highly beneficial and therapeutic activity for those, gardeners or not, who have or who develop a disability.

The basic principles of garden design still apply: deciding your needs, recognizing your local conditions and drawing up a plan, but if your mobility is restricted, the main consideration will be ease of access around the garden, so paths, steps and raised beds must be designed to make this as simple as possible. More paths will be needed than in a conventional garden and the additional cost shouldn't be underestimated. Bear in mind that in a small plot, several wide paths will reduce the area available for growing plants. One option is to have narrower paths with turning spaces at intervals and if done with attractive materials and in a regular fashion as part of the overall design of a garden, this can be striking. Examine carefully the characteristics of different materials to ensure that slipping isn't a

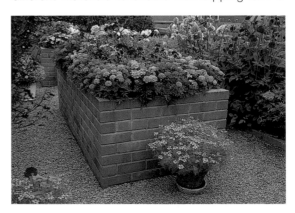

hazard. Some types of brick and paving are more slippery than others; decking is out. Loose gravel is difficult for wheelchair use but by using a 5mm/¼in layer of mechanically compacted chippings on top, the surface will be easier to grip. A low edging to a path will prevent wheelchairs from slipping off and is also useful to the visually impaired as a tapping rail.

Wide, shallow steps are the easiest to use but a slip-resistant surface is again important. Keep steps clear of obstacles such as plant pots and try to avoid positioning them under overhanging trees that drop fruit and leaves. A firm handrail can be helpful but do choose a style that fits in with the rest of the garden; there should be no reason to sacrifice aesthetics in the cause of functionality. Provided a slope is gradual, ramps can replace steps to keep costs down, but in positioning steps, try to work with the shape of the garden. Ramps are best made of concrete and the gradient should be at least 1:15; the ideal is 1:20. This does of course increase the length and in a small area, could be considered unsightly. Try to provide some screening or use a focal point therefore to draw the eye away from the ramp.

Raised beds are often advocated and do seem to make common sense but they are expensive to install, so, if you get the opportunity, try working with one in another garden first to satisfy yourself they really are what you want. If you do decide to go ahead, you have the option of free-standing raised beds or those built against an existing wall or slope. Free-standing beds are more expensive and look unnatural but access to both sides is possible. Cutting in to a slope and using a retaining wall to hold back the soil is cheaper and more attractive. Piling up soil against a garden wall and building a retaining wall in front is both quick and inexpensive and is worthwhile if you have an existing wall in a suitable position. A width of 60cm/24in (or 1.2m/4ft if there is to be access from both sides) is ideal for a raised bed but the most suitable height will depend on the height of the person using it and the types of tools they have. As a guide, assume that the shoulders are flat and the soil is below elbow level. The walls must be strong enough to hold the soil while being as thin as possible so the user can get close to the plants. Most raised beds are constructed from timber, concrete slabs or brick but weep holes may be needed for drainage and lining the inside with polythene can help to prevent damp from penetrating the materials.

An alternative to raised beds is to grow plants in containers on a level surface but do make sure that you have easy access to an outside tap or water butt. Many types of container are now available but half barrels are popular as they are large enough to grow a wide range of plants, inexpensive, fit into many gardening styles, can be left out overwinter and are firm and stable. Containers needn't be considered permanent fixtures, however, and can be moved on purpose-made trolleys which are readily available at garden centres and inexpensive. Hanging baskets and window boxes are also practicable for disabled gardeners, especially if a long handled sprayer or other device is used for ease of watering or, even better, they are fitted with a chain and pulley device – again, these are widely available.

CHILDREN IN THE GARDEN

Although it's design considerations on which I wish to concentrate, I always think that much of gardening with children is concerned with psychology. Be very careful with your 'don'ts' in the garden. Saying 'no' too frequently when children venture on to your own beds and borders will cause them to associate plants and gardening in general with something untouchable. It's far better to explain carefully why it is not a good idea to walk through the newly emerging seedlings or to play football with tomatoes.

Encouragement is the appropriate word with children, as most have relatively little patience and expect results both quickly and dramatically. I am convinced that setting aside a small area specifically for children's use is the ideal way to stimulate their interest. But don't be tempted to give them a spot in which you are unable to grow anything yourself; you should do quite the reverse. In the open garden, choose a place where the growing conditions are good, where the soil has already been well amended with organic matter and where there is good exposure to sunshine. An area of about 3.5–4m²/35–45 square feet will allow them plenty of scope although in a small garden, of course, this may need to be scaled down. Choose an area also that is close enough to a tap for the children not to have to carry cans of water long distances. I have often dated my own real passion for gardening to the day when, aged about seven, I beat my father in the onion-growing class at the village horticultural show; the reason I had managed to grow prize-winning onions at such a tender age was simply that I had been given, for my own garden, some of the best soil and growing conditions. I wasn't, like so many other children, expected to make do with a miserable and forsaken corner.

What are the types of plant most appealing to children? Hardy annuals raised from seed sown directly outside are almost always the most satisfactory, offering so much in return for so little. Vegetables are rewarding too for they offer something edible, although I am uncertain if, having grown spinach themselves, easy as it is, children will necessarily be more likely to eat it. Among other vegetables, radishes are the easiest of all, closely followed by lettuce (the small varieties such as 'Little Gem'), carrots (especially the quick growing early, spherical rooted types), peas, runner beans (which produce more dramatic results more quickly than almost any other vegetable), sweetcorn and courgettes. But almost all vegetables are worth trying and only space need really be the limiting factor. Among flowers, the list is longer still. Sunflowers are almost essential because of their astonishing size but candytuft, calendulas, nasturtiums, pansies, poppies, schizanthus, and ten-week stocks are all rewarding. When choosing seeds, however, either from a mail order catalogue or from a garden centre display, do allow your children some choice; there may be items that appeal to them from the pictures on the packets and only by trying them will they discover if they are easy or frustratingly difficult. It may also be worthwhile buying a few plants, partly to give them encouragement while their seeds germinate but also to demonstrate to children that some garden plants can only be propagated by cuttings; allowing them to take cuttings themselves will of course prove tremendous fun later.

So much for gardening with children. It is also important to consider gardening for children, especially those too young to understand even the basics of horticulture. The most important rule here must be a don't: don't have a garden pool (see page 100). Of course children also expect swings, sand pits, tree houses, rope ladders and similar essentials. But there's no reason why the entire garden should take on the appearance of a municipal playground. If the garden is large enough, set aside an area for play things, preferably an area visible from the house

(or, at least, from the kitchen) without being too obtrusive. Alternatively, choose items that can be put away easily and simply and that are made from materials that blend in with the environment. Children's garden equipment needn't be of luridly coloured plastic; relatively inexpensive wooden items are readily available. Nor need such features as sandpits be planned as permanent garden features; they may be constructed so they can be changed later into rock gardens, or even into pools.

AFTERWORD

Today's children will comprise the next gardening generation but no matter how enthusiastic they might be in their early formative years, whether their interest continues unabated through adolescence is in the hands of outside forces. It has been my experience that through the teenage years, an interest in gardening is unusual. Teenagers are, after all, generally more occupied with other things – including each other. But if that spark of interest has been laid in infancy, it will assuredly return once the young adult has his or her own first home. Admittedly, in today's economic climate, that first home is more likely to be an apartment than a house with the 'garden' simply a balcony or collection of houseplants; and it is likely to be rented rather than owned. None of this matters. Home is where your plants are and it is a relatively unusual home or human being that wants none. I was as surprised as I was delighted when my own elder son, now an army officer, discovered during his first term at the Royal Military Academy, Sandhurst, that he was required to have a house plant in his room. It was deemed, rightly I am sure, by the military authorities, that caring for some other living thing was an important aspect of a young officer's training. The image of a Sergeant Major inspecting the young officer cadet's begonias along with his bed linen and his boots is an endearing one.

But how much common sense will tomorrow's gardeners have? How good will they be at gardening and at coping with the challenges that plant care throws up? They are certainly exposed to more media outpourings and printed matter on gardening than any generation in history. My suspicion, however, is that while their horticultural taste buds may be tickled, they will be less well equipped actually to garden. While we learned by watching our parents and asking, today entertainment has taken the place of information. The sad irony is that, although we are now surrounded by the gardening industry and plant and equipment quality is generally very high, I doubt if the standard of home gardening as a craft has ever been lower. So there's a challenge for today's horticultural industry to take up, to set itself as a target – not simply higher sales of gardening goods (or, in many cases, of gardening trivia) but a real ambition simultaneously to educate and enthuse. Let's look for a little more common sense all round.

Editor Michael Brunström
Designer Caroline Clarke
Index Marie Lorimer
Production Kim Oliver